Penguin Books
Anna

ANNA

David Reed

Penguin Books

Penguin Books Ltd, Harmondsworth,
Middlesex, England
Penguin Books, 625 Madison Avenue,
New York, New York 10022, U.S.A.
Penguin Books Australia Ltd. Ringwood,
Victoria, Australia
Penguin Books Canada Ltd, 2801 John Street,
Markham, Ontario, Canada L3R 1B4
Penguin Books (N.Z.) Ltd, 182–190 Wairau Road,
Auckland 10, New Zealand

First published by Martin Secker & Warburg Ltd 1976

Published in Penguin Books 1977

The publishers gratefully acknowledge permission to quote
from the following:
The Divided Self by R. D. Laing, published by Tavistock
Publications Limited, London;
Burns and their Treatment by I. F. K. Muir and T. L.
Barclay (first edition 1962), published by Lloyd-Luke
(Medical Books) Limited, London.

Made and printed in Great Britain by
C. Nicholls & Company Ltd,
Set in Monotype Times

Contents

Part One

Facing Madness

1

The diary opens on 2 May 1973. A friend had invited us to dinner, but Anna didn't feel up to it. I suppose, as so often before, I sensed inwardly what was coming and my spirit, my body, cried out to escape

So I went alone.

A day passed, marked in the diary only by 'floor tiles and M S corrections'. It was the day Anna normally went to her psychiatrist.

On Friday she went again – for the third time that week. She was nervous, on edge, and had been typing away in her study above the garden for days – things she had written in longhand in the weeks before and now committed to type:

'You' took me away from David.
'You' want to destroy him – David, my 'child', whom I sought/feared to destroy.

This was dated 1 May 1973, at the top of a sheaf of typescript papers which I discovered some five months later in the room – a chronology of self-examination, conducted alone; a struggle of selves that could not be stilled – that urged towards greater insight, to deeper lucidity.

I got the material on Friday – dark first, then bright, not for myself, but for furnishing. Madras cotton, refined Indian style. I had long wanted to do away with Margo's cover for my settee, and then the worn Persian carpets from my mother-in-law. I wanted my own sitting-room.

I had been rearranging pictures before, family pictures, my sons, my husband, my father – I put dried roses up for my father's grave, but removed the picture back to the others, or with the others for the first time. I put up a little drawing my aunt made, a farm-house in fact, a

9

house – that's what she went for, that's what I went for – a house, possibly a home.

I had bought some cheap material previously – for a shirt for my elder son, Gabriel, I thought – or a dress (apron-dress!) for myself. But then I chose the sophisticated Indian one – I am fed-up with being the simpleton of the family, the girl who can't keep her children clean, the girl who can't make her husband happy. Did they try to keep me down ('in my place') by going to a shopgirl's shop for my wedding dress, by refusing access to Laing when David asked for it? Did they find me a convenient scapegoat? Did I lend myself for it? Sure I did – but did they really know their son? Are they not still hating me for having crossed their plans? I sacrificed my first child to them, but that seems not enough. The millionaire's daughter, Elizabeth, anybody in the right position – but not me.

Anna had dated this – or rather the original – End April, 1973.

There was also the draft of a letter she intended to write to her previous consultant at the psychiatric hospital – a letter apologizing for having given up her therapy there after only a year to go to her own private therapist. She had never explained this to the hospital: now she felt a sense of guilt – and perhaps even something more – for in the bottom left-hand corner of the page she had written in biro:

Why should I want to see the consultant at my old hospital at this point?

Poor Anna! She knew, I suppose, what she was in for. Her old consultant would have sensed her alarm, her mounting nervousness; would have prescribed drugs, possibly a period in hospital; would have protected her from herself. Yet in going to a private psychiatrist – a man recommended by R. D. Laing – she had now chosen to confront this self, however disturbing. In part Anna's typewritten papers were for him – a dialogue.

Nor was I the only loved-one in question. Anna's dissatisfaction with me related directly to the feelings she bore for this new psychiatrist, at once intimate and distant: a relationship which in turn called up the spectre of the only lover she had known since meeting me – a fellow student at the university in Munich whose ghost now came back to haunt her.

10

Dream – the day before our sitting-room was laid out, the night we threw the old, dirty carpet out, the night after I cleared the drains, and dusted the bedroom.

I was with Christoph. I met him at an exhibition. The dream before, at the same place, a girl had kissed me (a girl like Elizabeth, David's German friend, a girl like a girl I once knew at school). I drove home with Christoph, towards home. We were very happy, there was no sex, but the feeling as though we might have had sex. I knew I was going back to David and the two boys. It was evening, about 6–8. I would say I was at my therapist's, but the therapist was not you, but the one from the psychiatric hospital. After the dream I thought that David without his family (father) would have stood no chance against Christoph: I went to Christoph at night, before my last breakdown in Munich. I always felt my mother had rather pushed me into marrying David (like my grandmother is said by my mother to have pushed her second daughter, the artist, into marrying – my mother hates and despises that man). But on the other hand, Christoph was not prepared to marry me, he wanted me to grow up *first* – I thought, after the dream, I would write all those essays I carry about in my mind for Christoph, suddenly assuming he would not be married, also knowing I would probably not leave my children. Christoph I really loved – but when I saw him again, time had elapsed, he had not come to see me in hospital, though he wanted to – friends (I wonder who) thought it would confuse me – I had got yellow roses from David's mother, and red roses from David – and I saw Christoph on his bike and did not call out for him.

Now he is Dr Rathgens and works for the Bavarian radio. Munich was narrow. I lived in a narrow room with a tiny grey window for seven years. When I first broke down in this country I thought David's father would send me back into the grey nothingness of my student room. Christoph was still a student when I knew him. I would not feel so guilty (for marrying David) but for the episode with Christoph – the only one I have had sex with since I met David, ten years ago (from now!).

At the bottom of the sheet – undated – Anna had added:

But I could, of course, have been very much attracted by Christoph and yet decided to marry David – maybe the two are not/were never real alternatives – one would have been for some time, the other is for life. Did I really have another few years to waste, at the age of 26, *if I wanted children?*

2

That Friday evening I had tickets for the World Theatre at the Aldwych; again Anna didn't feel like going, and I took a friend. The play was a farce. Anna had deeper preoccupations.

Giving Juliette the book I presented myself to my mother – a free and adventurous self. Juliette for me has the attraction of beautiful horses, of a horse which knows its value, not the softness of Ulme, the gypsy horse. Ulme was a lost soul, Marilies was a lost soul, there was no difference. Kirsi by contrast was coy, despite all her tenderness, she insisted on distance.

Anna had never quite been able to forgive Juliette for entering my life as she had done, for loving me in her own apparently untouchable way; and ever since Anna had tried to come to terms with her, with her own envy, her dislike, her contempt and her bitterness. As they were both interested in child education Anna had given Juliette a book to read: it was her way of trying to make up, to say, 'I still resent you, but I want you to know that I admire you also, would want you as a friend if all this had not happened'. Juliette was many things to Anna: 'a free and adventurous self' as Anna put it, the self she could never liberate. It was useless my telling Anna how unhappy, how frustrated and unfulfilled Juliette really was – as I knew. It was what Juliette signified in her terms that preoccupied Anna – the names of her other school and university friends, of little boyish Kirsi – our Finnish au pair girl of the year before – they show how Anna was attempting to coordinate her feelings, her sensitivity, her relationships – to reach a kind of existential understanding.

I was once soft and malleable. David wants me to become hard – but it only gets as far as a symbolic amulet, such as Hilda once wore. Aunt Hilda never did anything for me, nothing; yet she was there at least. She had her little attic room, and she stitched me a blouse, and a Russian tunic for my brother Berthold. My mother couldn't even sew me a nightdress – is that the reason she showers pyjamas on David now?

Grandma used to carry the water down the stairs backwards; she did everything for us, impossible to know what she had missed with her own children. Grandpa built the waterstands; otherwise was a tyrant. Force of will and punctuality – and he hated the peasants, the farming people, as if he hadn't come from the country himself. Aunt Helga poured her life into verse which left out what was important, and Ann, Aunt Ann, hoarded money to buy herself a little house. It appears only the youngest one managed to find a real path. No one spoke of Heinrich in his lunatic asylum, probably least of all his ambitious brother. They had once come from Salzburg, and were proud of it, proud of their faith, proud of their unbendable strength. But the birch bends in the wind, the proud oak bends – Penthesilea is after all a tragedy, not an example to be followed.

I wore brown suede shoes and unassuming colours, and knew that elegance was not for me. Towards Ludwig I would have had to become hard; so I found an escape by choosing a masculine type, even though he was still a boy then. My father was soft, my mother became hard; my aunt Hilda remained a girl for a long time, but at least she has no exaggerated feelings. My grandmother was generous, perhaps extravagant. In old age she was good and full of understanding. We all make mistakes; a few of us come in time to see them ...

Anna had dated this 27 April 73. It was written and typed in German with only a few English phrases – whereas most of the other papers were written entirely in English. She wanted to understand: to see where and how the mistakes in her life, her family's life, had come from – had led or misled her.

3

I woke up masturbating.
I still felt the weight of my child's presents round my arm.
The presents are laid out,
exactly,
ready to be unwrapped.
Tomorrow is Gabriel's birthday,
And I am still in London
masturbating with/for my bloody therapist
David next to me ill
and I sit up and drink tea

writing a love poem for my bloody therapist –
actually I found him catlike today
unmanly in his movements
because he rejects me.
Masturbating with
or masturbating for
das ist hier die Frage
c'est ici la question
this is the question.
I could murder you for your stupid questions
not even questions, just blankness
sexy or erotic
English or German.
Madam, it's the same the world over
love-mate
Don't call me madam, please,
I said to the shopgirl
who looked like a boy.
This time I sent the letter to Kirsi,
the girl I always write to
when I'm in love with you.
I wanted to go to Oman with her
take photographs of children
young boys
and men on camel back.
I wanted to go to Oman
to study life there
where it would not be threatening.
But in fact I'm going to Crete
and quite happy to get away
and perhaps some shepherd or other
might teach me how to play the flute.

We had planned to go to Crete – or rather, I had planned for us
to go. It had taken two years to research and write my most recent
book, and during this time I had taken only a week's holiday –
and that on a racing yacht which frightened me. I needed, as
Anna needed, to get right away; and I had in mind a book about
Minoan and modern Crete. I had prepared a synopsis while
finishing the biography: I was waiting only for my agent to find a
publisher willing to commission it.

But Anna was never really keen on the idea. We had had a violent tussle at Christmas when my parents gave me a cheque for £100 towards a spring holiday, and a handful of brochures. We had toyed with the idea of going to Tunisia or Morocco – until Anna announced she did not really want to go on holiday with me at all.

I remember my anger at this. I was upset, for the more Anna's psychoanalysis and my own writing kept us separate, the more I dreamed of our finding love again in some distant land. Anna's rejection went right through me – I tore up the brochures in a passion, and wept bitterly within. Yet a part of me knew that Anna needed to be away from me to exist at all, that she suffocated within the framework of my existence.

One awakes to the sad truth: one has used each other for one's own purposes. I wanted to get away from my mother who was driving me into madness, wanted to enter the strong-man family as protection against my mother, and with the mythical figure of the General in the background – a grandfather figure, perhaps a reminder of the time with my own grandfather, which I saw as rosy – rosy in comparison with the period when I was exposed alone to my mother.

David wanted to get away from his father, from his father's expectations, from his father's world; and I was the counter-world. When I first met him he had no personality of his own really. The Director and the General: they flowed into one river and had as their effluence a boy named David. His world blinded me, and he was carefree enough to take me out of an imprisoning or untenable situation – only to return to his castle and write me moralizing letters with crests on the notepaper: General's Residence. I recognized I was beaten ...

As it is I did not get him away from his father, nor did he get me away from my mother.

This was dated Easter 1973 – though like the other sheets I think Anna typed it out in those first days in May.

Then came the matter of the child.

4

Which night it happened I no longer know, but during the week preceding 6 May, Anna became convinced that she was pregnant. She had forgotten to take the pill, and we had made love: it was enough to convince her she had conceived.

Days elapsed before she told me. It is curious that I noted nothing in my diary about this. For Saturday I have only: 'Invited to Laurie and May's for Monday night. Wet. Neighbours' children came round. Anna asleep in afternoon for $3\frac{1}{2}$ hours. Cup Final.' And for Sunday: 'Wet again.' The question, the tortured question of the child, exploded in our lives – and yet I did not mention it. I must ask myself why.

Everyday work should be done (disposed of) as simply and with as little effort as possible ... but first there are the symbolic stocks which have to be cleared: e.g. first present for Satu, the au pair (Juliette = Mother), a toy which I really bought for myself; second present for Satu (Juliette = Mother), writing paper, analogous to that which I had bought for myself; third present for Satu: a bunch of flowers, for Easter – and also because they were cheaper, and different from the ones I bought myself; the first unsymbolic present.

Whereas I *had to* buy the cat basket (Helen), to stop the cat sleeping in my children's pram. I don't want to see the pram again; I don't want to be continually reminded – of what?

Amory will have the highchair

Eugenie the sheets

the nappies I have given to Carole.

Anna was deviously determined to get at the truth. She wanted to separate her symbolic longings from reality. But in the growing torment of her mind questions of family, children, our pram, a baby – they mounted towards that most revolutionary of symbols: the birth of a new child.

For a while Anna attempted – as if sensing this – to refine her whole self-analysis with radical, searing honesty; by going back even to the period before I first met her, to the time she intended to marry Ludwig Mecklenburg, her German Baron.

Did I want the children?

Did I want this husband?

I had slotted myself into the Mecklenburg family. I did not have the strength to start a family of my own. But: Ludwig was too weak to hold me. What was concealed behind the break-up, my quest for freedom?

Archetypally the flight from mother to father, and my brother involved there too; David came as knight with sword. I am still afraid to be alone; I still seek maternal approval.

These children are my own; the aborted child was Ludwig's. I knew it was a son; and to sew even a pair of trousers for Gabriel becomes both a problem and a symbolic act: the whole confusion was either first released by David or at any rate became exposed through him; possibly as Mecklenburg-painter's wife the confusion would have been shelved (for a while) – though the idea that I should earn money and Ludwig paint makes one wonder.

Of course, it looks rosy with hindsight, my bringing up the child under the protection of Mother Mecklenburg; Ludwig and I possibly both living in his room (studio). In reality the child would have been given to the mother to look after, enabling me to go out and earn money. Whose child . . . ?

. . . or my mother might have wanted to take the child so that I could go on studying; there never would have been such a thing as my own child.

Even Gabriel was not my child; he was produced to beat off the (grand) parents; in my own words he looked like 'Daddy' and 'David's brother', Stephen. In David archetypally, I married my child; how could he be the father? In fact, I made him *into* my child, and my son into my lover and/or consoler – whilst also stylizing him into a repetition of my self. The start of change, of correction, lies not with the child but with the father – the father I am running away from.

> running away to my mother
> running away to my father
> running away to Ludwig.

There was a blank space after this; and then, right at the very bottom of the page, Anna had typed: 'I am quite simply running away. Perhaps I chose him too to be my mother, but more probably I am running away from a human reality.'

And on the next page:

Neither father nor mother
neither brother nor son
simply my husband
    my husband I am not satisfied with
    not the way he speaks
    not his way with the children
    not his way of touching me
this man, who is my husband, has no right to touch me –
Madam, then he cannot be your husband.

It was dated 21 April 1973. There followed a poem in German:

Competing with journalists
seven years to build a home, marriage, family
seven years before that at the university
where I, if not in the wrong place
was at any rate completely displaced.
Faulty attitudes.
The last seven years helped, among other things,
to find the therapist
with whom I'm stuck.
Well, well, *one makes one's own decisions,*
even in therapy.
I read sociological texts, as explanation, protest;
my only worthwhile act:
giving a man in prison hope.
Art.
I turned away from her, hated her, denied her.
The academic. The practical.
David rescued me from literary science,
from David's hold I must now free myself.
Djuna Barnes – this study *must* be written.
The first seven years brought David's biography
the second seven will bring Djuna Barnes.
Then children again.

But then the desire for a third child had become more immediate,
and the idea of writing a book about Djuna Barnes was set aside
in the gathering tension. The letter to our old au pair, Kirsi,
puts Anna's quest for independence very simply – merely dated
April:

Dear Kirsi,

David has finished his book, and I am left in utmost depression. For he has already got his next plans at hand: to go to Crete, take photographs there (with a photographer) and prepare a sort of poetical book on the island. We should all come along. Fine, except that I feel like a camel following his master's steps. Also, I am a bit jealous, for the photographer is, of course, a girl. 'Take this shot, and that ...' Well, you see, I wouldn't be prepared to do that. I'd have my own ideas (I hope she will have her own ideas too; but then he respects it more in strangers than in his own wife. Maybe my own ideas threaten him, maybe I threaten him, and so I have to be kept down, or that is what it feels like).

I was in Germany not long ago. There I had ideas of my own – I undug an old essay I had done, on Southern Arabia, and I thought I'd like to go there and study the people. I've always been interested in anthropology (literature has in a way been knocked out of my hand; David hates academics and academic interpretation, and German academics in particular). But last year, staying with friends, I even expressed the hope I had of writing some essays on literature of my own, but as soon as I am alone with David – or am just alone – my head feels empty. Maybe I wouldn't get anywhere on my own either, maybe ... yes, now I remember: a colour test I used to do every so often, seeing whether I had changed – invariably the result came to something like: feels threatened by other people, fears that others stop her from doing her own thing. Well, during therapy it has rather been established that it is myself who stops me doing my own thing, executing my plans, pursuing my ideas. It is simply easier to blame others. But the main thing should not be to blame at all, but to see what it is that prevents me from doing what I should like to do, how I prevent myself, and for what reasons. Fear. Fear of failing, even fear of having to try hard.

Dear Kirsi, I have often been thinking of you, I missed you very much when you had left. I had one girlfriend a bit like you and I have never heard from her again once she left Munich; I would feel poorer if the same would happen with you. It is difficult having girlfriends once you are married, but that is exactly it: I sometimes feel, women have also a world of their own to share, and they should not give it up.

The letter ends there; and was evidently sent, for only the carbon remains. What Kirsi made of it I cannot tell.

It is the last of the typescripts that I found. There remain only a series of brief handwritten messages written on mauve cards with

19

matching envelopes. But they belong to a slightly different period. Possibly they were written on Monday 7 May. The two addressed to her mother were marked ominously above the address on the front: 'Beware, dynamite – I cannot help it.' And on the back: 'P.S. Let Berthold free!'

5

The question of pregnancy became more urgent that week-end, and I tried to reason with Anna. I asked her why she should want another child now, in the midst of her therapy when it was questionable whether she would be able to give it the love and freedom we both felt a child needs. She said that our first child, Gabriel, had been an accident, that our second, Thomas, she had wanted but I not: now was the moment to have a child we *both* desired.

I didn't know what to say. After the years of labour on my book a part of me yearned just for love and domestic happiness; and it is no exaggeration to say that children represented the symbol, the confirming extension of my love for Anna. It was true that I hadn't been anxious to have a second child (for reasons to be explained later); but once it was established that Anna was pregnant, I had found myself curiously contented, and came to love him as deeply as I did Gabriel.

But a third child to cope with at home? In the context of Anna's increasing nervousness and intensity all that week, I shied from it. I had no knowledge of the papers Anna was writing, nor had she told me anything about them; but I knew she was upset, and was troubled. And the issue of the child seemed so very much an escape, an outlet, a convenient exit – and one which at a certain level I longed to share: a sort of romantic '*je m'en fou*' to the world, a statement of love, of hope and faith amid the constant pressures and oppressions of outside.

I talked it over with Anna; asked whether she had discussed it with her psychiatrist; but she said no, it had not come up – something I found almost incredible considering that she had been to him three times that week, and that it was uppermost in her mind. As regards the factual question whether she had conceived I suggested we go and see our doctor the next day, Monday, as I had no idea myself how the pill actually worked and what happened if you missed it.

Whether, then, it was my disinclination to run into a new pregnancy blind – especially *after* the event! – that further upset Anna, I cannot tell; but after the weeks of brave examination of herself and our situation in her documents and letters she now launched into missives which leave no doubt how close she was to breaking point. She dated only one of them. It was addressed to me:

David,

You have to go to Crete, but I cannot come with you. If you think of Elizabeth, do it now, because she is about to leave that man.

She had dated this 3 May 1973. The other cards were written in a different coloured ink several days later:

Dear Mother,

I cannot accept any cut flowers from you, at least not at the moment. I do not yet understand why. But I won't let the money-voucher lapse . . .

You chose an unfortunate day to ring, and to be quite honest I am not in the least interested with whom you spent Easter or any other holidays. Perhaps one day . . . but at the moment I have enough myself to consider, and *my* family . . .

And whether you go to Istanbul or Sicily – good heavens, that is your own affair – stop burdening your children with it. I find it bad enough that you patronize your sister Hilda in all the rules of art, and make sarcastic remarks about her husband in the presence of her daughter – that you give her work I find good and honourable, but one has to separate the two. And in the end it's of no shitting importance to me how much money my children have in their savings bank – if it gives you satisfaction, well then, please: but keep it to yourself. At the moment my children are suffering from the distress of their mother – that is what counts.

Anna

But this was not all. There was a second envelope, marked 'II'; and on it in pencil Anna had scribbled 'Sorry again' in her dazzlingly fine but racing script. It was once more to her mother.

As regards Hilda, she hardly did anything in Lüneberg – but she did make me a blouse and a Russian tunic for Berthold. You made sure we didn't starve – but there are different kinds of hunger. And Siegmund – Siegmund did in the end buy her the house by the water, and the court case then was possibly more or less a way, an opportunity, of standing up for once to the elder sister . . . Not everyone can conform to the official boundaries of age – and he didn't exactly have things *easy* either. Instead of ironic remarks such as 'poor' – I didn't want to put it so harshly, but it's true. Enough on that subject.

As far as my own husband is concerned, it was you who once *pushed* me into marriage – I myself had very divided *feelings*. It took a long, long time for me to realize that the other man was a wrong turning – your behaviour and attitude showed concern (and fear), but nothing of trust and respect for the individual rights of others, even your own daughter. I can say it *now*, after having dragged it for seven years through our marriage. Mother, if you wish to find yourself, it is getting late . . . You chose work, the way you were; and as things stood then, you hardly had any alternative. You chose work and the security of possessions. But it is not too late to transform money and property from a burden into a blessing, and I'm sure you are on the way to that. However, your children must not be bound by this property – I am forcing myself free. Berthold, like Papa, is dutiful. He feels in the same way responsible for you as Papa did for Grandma – he too feels you have had a hard life. But I know that also, have no fear, I know it only too well. And I know too that you made up to others what you didn't manage with me. But one good deed is not enough. Some people are helped with money – myself, in fact, for my therapy. David has done enough for the moment by marrying me, giving me children and now even a home. I cannot expect him at present to cough up the money for my therapy as well – and I am not in a position to earn it myself at the moment (David will simply break down if I force him to *earn* money now) – *and I do not want his father's money*. Mother – you can give me the money – you would be giving it not only to me but to the children; and David in the end a wife who can be a real wife to him. Berthold – Berthold needs something else – justice is not equal shares for everyone, but to each according to his *need*. Birgit – I know in some ways she is more similar to you than to me. Perhaps that is the reason you don't like her. Accepting oneself – I needed a mother, Birgit needs a man, a husband who belongs to her, not to her mother-in-law.

I shall do what I can for her, as far as I am physically able, but at heart she needs Berthold – and he needs her, not you.

Enough for today.

Your grown-up daughter

These letters were never sent. Instead, on Monday morning we went to see our G P. I have checked the appointment. It was for 7 May 1973, at 11 a.m.

6

Anna began to cry and the doctor asked what was the trouble. I felt embarrassed because Anna's weeping humiliated me some-how, suggesting that we were unhappy. It was this pride of mine, this unwillingness to involve others in our own private dilemmas which – well, that must come later.

Not that the doctor wished to be involved. In his own way he was a model doctor, thorough and intelligent. Yet his view of medicine stopped where psychology began. Medicine was for him a professional, practical world. Around it you built your family and social life, made friends with patients, used them and helped them. But you didn't ask questions; and psychology for him meant questions.

I explained what had happened – or what Anna thought had happened. He gave a brief account of how the pill worked and the unlikelihood of conception having taken place. Anna became very quiet.

'But it's not like you to miss your tablets, Anna,' he remarked. 'You take your Stellazine and Toffanil pills regularly, don't you?'

Anna answered that she was taking no drugs at the moment.

He looked quizzical. 'But when you do take them, you take them regularly. Did you *want* to miss the pill? Is it that you *want* to have another baby?'

Anna began to cry again. The following day she would break down and a course of events would be set in motion that was to

23

end in tragedy. Yet having asked that question and seen Anna's distress in reply, he looked down at his notes, and then back at me.

'I think the rest is a marital problem,' he said curtly. I led Anna, weeping, outside.

I took Anna home – shy woman whom I loved, yet was so little able to help. According to my diary she was 'nervous' all that day, and flung many 'accusations' against my parents. In the evening we went to the Herberts'.

I don't think Anna wished to go; but I insisted. As on the evening I went to Helen's, I felt a great need to get away from our house, to escape its tension. Yet, as it had with Helen, the evening went badly and led to bitter argument.

Perhaps I had looked forward to it too much. I was always glad to see Laurie. I liked his infectious laugh, his almost school-boy mistrust of people and situations, his constant need for reassurance and yet his probing independence in matters of the mind.

May was tall, with a squarish, handsome face and dark hair, fringed. She spoke with an impediment; and she tended to screw up her eyes and laugh loudly while thinking.

Anna was very quiet, and we had to wait a long time for dinner as the oven had broken and the meal had to be cooked in the lodger's flat below. I tried to get Anna to talk about the baby-question and what was happening in her therapy. Laurie was strangely sympathetic, on the same wavelength.

Then over the meal we had a violent argument about Nixon and the Watergate. I found myself taking a conservative, scep-tical view of the whole affair – that the silent majority wished to be blind to the truth not only out of materialistic preoccupations but also because they doubted politically whether a more honest system could be devised in their country. I suppose in fact I was talking about Anna.

Laurie became furious. He claimed I was condoning what had happened, that there were probably far worse revelations to come, and that Nixon would not stop short of murder if it was a question of avoiding his own ruin – and instanced Nixon's ruth-less bombing of Hanoi to speed up negotiations, much as Lyndon

Johnson had supposedly arranged for Kennedy's assassin to be murdered. At that we became very vehement.

Later we went to Laurie's study while Anna talked to May. Laurie showed me some of his new poems; and finally at Anna's insistence we left at 1.30 a.m. It was Anna's last night of sanity before she broke down.

7

She awoke sometime after 5 a.m. agitated. Her appointment with the psychiatrist was for 4 o'clock in the afternoon; but 'by then' my diary records, 'so nervous that she asked if I would come with her. Already very anti-social – met Diana T. on train for example, Anna staring at her, hardly talking.'

We got out of the train, handed in the tickets, and walked to the steps that led down to the Underground station below. Suddenly, before we even reached the ticket office or the automatic machines, Anna balked. She could go no further.

Her dark eyes looked haunted by terror. Her whole body revolted. No matter how much I tried to comfort her, to convince her that she need have no fear, she couldn't overcome it. She was suddenly convinced that my father – and the C I A – were having us followed, and would corner us in the Underground. She was certain we were being watched; she cowered, near to tears. It was then I knew, if I had not already recognized it on the train, that something irremediable had begun, that there could be no turning back. A dam had burst – and I couldn't run away. I was not frightened myself. Yet I knew then that those past three years of relative stability were over – that there was no going back, and that the awful pain of witnessing, of experiencing another human being's madness was beginning. There was no question of taking her home at that moment: only of the quickest way to reach Landis, the psychiatrist.

I suggested we take a taxi; but Anna was sure that we would be followed. She kept repeating the same fears about my father, then clutching me, terrified, looking into my eyes and asking whether

I was 'with' her. Even persuading her to take the bus with me was difficult.

We were late. I went in with her. Landis was waiting in his consulting-room. No furniture, only cushions and a coarse cord carpet – new – which was very slightly too large for the room; some piles of medical literature; and on the mantelpiece some small card-file cabinets. Anna immediately went up to them and began looking for her name. Landis assured her, from where he sat cross-legged on the other side of the room, that it wasn't among them.

Anna became very excited. She wouldn't sit down on the black cushions but kept striding about the room, and then lying down and crossing her arms behind her head. Suddenly she pulled herself up. And out of her slim, apparently empty white cloth shoulder-bag she pulled the green and black silk trouser-suit and earrings my father had brought her from his recent visit to the Far East, and threw them down in front of Landis, saying contemptuously, 'Trash, trash! What do you think of this?'

Landis, rather astonished, leaned forwards from his Buddha-like position and unfolded the suit. He held it up rather lovingly, admiringly, so delicately it might have been lingerie; then refolded it gently so as not to crease it or leave any tab buttons undone on the blouse. Meanwhile he said nothing.

Anna, like a conjuror, now produced a further item from the 'empty' bag. This was even more astonishing to me as I had travelled with her all the way from home and had no idea she had it. It was a German edition of Chairman Mao's Little Red Book which my father had also brought back for her – and Anna threw it in front of Landis silently but as if to say: 'Look how he makes fun of me!'

As Landis quietly refolded the silk suit, Anna suddenly got up and went for a glass of water – as though the intensity of these thoughts, these nervous exclamations, pacings, conjurings, had completely dehydrated her.

While she was out Landis eyed me in his half-distant, half-penetrating way, almost daringly:

'Does it scare you?'

But he didn't know what had happened at the Underground

station, that it went much deeper than a slightly overwrought session. I said, To be honest, no, it didn't scare me, since I had witnessed Anna behaving like this before, but that it was none-theless difficult to cope with – both because of her hysteria and also because her vituperation, aimed so directly against my parents, was thus indirectly pointed at me.

But it wasn't long before this itself was corrected. Before I had finished speaking to Landis, Anna returned from the bathroom with a glass of water: and started on me. I was but a pawn of my father, an 'eighty-year-old', a man already old and concerned with success in his writing solely in order to satisfy the expecta-tions, the hopes of his father.

I protested that this wasn't fair, quoted my friend Peter as an instance of the opposite – Peter, who was at Cambridge with me, whose marriage had failed and whose deep artistic potential had never been fulfilled: for Peter had truly wanted to stay within the orbit of his father and had never broken that parental hold.

But Anna was in no mood to be contradicted – nor did it invalidate her point.

Somehow, if I think now about her challenge – since that is what it was for me, however I might try to wriggle out – was it not there, then, in that confrontation before the psychiatrist with his straggly hair and glazed yet penetrating eyes and nervous, birdlike gestures, that everything that followed was fixed? Yet Landis had apparently little notion of what was going on. In my diary I wrote: 'How can R.L. let us go away without offering to see us/Anna/me before Thursday if necessary? Does he not *realize* the gravity now?'

But it was also my own pride that stopped me, as it did throughout the following months, from insisting. Anna had somehow thrust down, with the Chinese suit and earrings and the Little Red Book, a kind of gauntlet to me, the 'eighty-year-old' biographer, the pawn and dupe of a successful father. I felt that she was being unfair to me, but that she wasn't wrong – at least not in her own terms and perception. By deferring to Landis – by slipping out of my own responsibility here to prove myself and my love to her – I would be showing that she was right. Perhaps, too, I was envious of this strange, small fellow, sitting cross-legged, who attracted so much of Anna's own affection and longing.

Whatever the motives, I took Anna home with my mind made up: that I wouldn't fail her, that I would now stand by her whatever might come. I was aware, deeply aware, that Landis had let her down, us down. A woman, his patient for almost two years now, had come to him in obvious distress; he had treated her as though her state was no different from what it had been in any other week or session, and had allowed her to go away without any special concern. It was to be a fortnight before he seemed to recognize how serious the case had become and offered advice and help: and by then that part of me which was ready to share the true problem of Anna's insanity had become embittered and hostile.

8

We made love that night – for there at least I could show the wonder and affection and delight I felt for her, spiritually and no less physically. But afterwards Anna would not sleep. She kept getting up and wandering, and then returning to the bed to lie awake beside me, too excited, too intense to contemplate relaxation or sleep. Her dark brown eyes became searingly bright; she didn't talk, but seemed totally preoccupied with what was going on inside her.

It was now Wednesday. At nine I took Gabriel to school. When I returned Anna was setting out a sort of exhibition in the bedroom. I realized that in her nocturnal pacing she had been assembling a number of items which reflected or triggered off her inner preoccupations: knives, postcards, newspaper pages with certain headlines and stories ringed and underlined in red biro: Peter Niesewand's 'fear' in prison; his concern for 'prisoners he left behind'. There was also a story I had seen myself in *The Times* and sought to conceal, about twins, aged four, drowning in a ditch.

'Twins seem to be very much at issue here,' I entered in my diary. 'She has Stephen's Persian jewel-box out against my own from India' – a reference to the gift my twin brother had brought her from Persia one summer while we were engaged, and the element of rivalry it had suddenly introduced into our fraternal relationship. I had been so unsure of Anna then; and Stephen's independence, his intellectual openness, his lack of seriousness must have had a lot of charm against my own suffering longing.

'Poor Satu [the Finnish au pair] very frightened by it, I think – and Thomas [our 2½-year-old] clinging to me, insisting on my presence.'

Satu wisely concealed all the remaining sharp knives in the house; but it was not only Satu and the children who were upset and frightened by Anna's sudden change. At lunchtime Helen rang to ask if Anna could translate a publisher's blurb from German (something Anna had done for her before). I tried to explain that Anna was unwell; but Helen didn't appear to understand, and came over a few minutes later. Anna stared at her hostilely, and Helen fled. Then in the afternoon another friend, Pepita, came with her little boy who was the same age as Thomas – and again Anna said nothing, but either looked distant, indifferent, or stared hostilely. Pepita, though a journalist and much interested in educational and social problems, tried bravely to look unperturbed, but left within an hour at 4.15. 'Children not happy with each other either,' I noted. 'Anna goes upstairs, and I take the children to the playground in the park – with their friends from round the corner – in relief at being able to get away and to show love for them without it being spurned.

'Exhausted after walk I make them supper and they go straight to bed. Anna becomes completely silent with me now, talking to me only in gestures, symbols – clutching my face, my hands, touching the ring, etc. – and alas – I am too tired and frightened to respond! I try to ring Roy Landis – at 10.30 as it turns out – and then realize how ridiculous, frightened and impatient I am being.'

It was becoming, as I also noted in the diary, 'a case of lasting out till Thursday', the time of Anna's next appointment with Landis. But if I thought about it, I had no confidence that Landis would do or say anything. He would only spring the whole question back at me.

It was therefore I who had to learn to cope with this situation. Yet how was I to cope?

We went up to bed, where Anna's symbolic gesturing became a kind of grotesque sexual initiation. Her movements became rigid, coarse; her eyes wild. In my diary I described her behaviour as 'aggressive, smelly – she has, in her symbol-talk, put her hand under her skirt and tights and daubed my forehead with vaginal odour, saying that it was only this that I needed, not the "rest" '. She began clutching at me, insisting that we 'fuck' – and I was frightened. 'This aggressive grabbing of my balls and body I find ugly, disconcerting, and turn away from her. Is this wrong?'

Was it? Who can know or even imagine the sensations that occur when your own wife, normally so shy, quiet, sensitive, undemonstrative, so inhibited sexually, goes insane and tears at you, your sexual organs and your flesh? Of course, it was my own fault for so continually shelving a confrontation with Anna, with her problems, with *our* problems: I wanted her in the image that I revered and which aroused me. I had, in fact, caged Anna: and now, like an animal which turns on its keeper – and who knows? perhaps unconsciously that was the role-situation Anna was acting out for me, to me – she turned the tables: and I was afraid.

I turned away; and in fear I slept. But Anna did not sleep.

9

Anna was not to sleep at all for several weeks. At times, when I could find sufficient strength to think dispassionately of what was happening to us, I would be brought to tears at the recollections of that 'first' day at Landis's, the magician's performance with the Chinese silk suit – a kind of black comedy, yet profoundly moving: for one of the things that made me love Anna so dearly was just this ability to surprise, to astonish people – most of all me. And nothing could have been more astonishing than that afternoon.

But that way of thinking was confined to moments of optimism – or at any rate to moments when I was ready for anything that might happen and could still laugh, still see irony in the chaos. The rest was in deadly earnest.

Thursday morning dawned, with Anna still dressed. 'I manage to get Gabriel to school all right, then collect prescription for sleeping tablets. Get Anna to take 2, try to keep her upstairs to relax, though still she doesn't sleep,' I wrote. 'She has become utterly silent and withdrawn now, like a "patient".'

Satu told me that morning that she was frightened, and I wondered how long she would stay if things didn't get better. For her it must have been so much more dramatic and threatening than for me: a quiet, shy girl speaking very little English, not particularly intelligent, who suddenly witnesses the mistress of the house becoming insane – and the master not 'doing' anything about it.

In fact I was doing all I could. I had stopped work completely, and was determined now to see Anna through this breakdown if I possibly could. And even if it did get worse – what was impossible really? If I had been working in a regular 9 to 5 job away from home I would, paradoxically, have had no choice but to go to our G P and make sure that Anna was hospitalized; yet my very life as a writer gave me the time – particularly now that the manuscript was completed – to keep Anna at home and see her through the breakdown, with all its attendant risks. Our plight arose from who we were and from the past that had formed so much of us. We began to see a future: but to get to it there had to be this journey through Hades.

For a second time, on the afternoon of 10 May 1973, I accompanied Anna on the journey to see her psychiatrist. She was utterly silent, though she had eaten the lunch I had made – her first food for three days, since our meal at Laurie and May's. I drove her in our camper van. She sat in the back, staring through the windows. We got there early, and I took Anna to a restaurant where she drank some tea. Then we drove on to Landis's.

Landis appeared at 4 p.m. but didn't seem to want me to be present. I said I would go for a walk, and returned just after five. Anna hadn't moved from the kitchen; nor had she spoken.

Yet still Landis refused to involve me. Whether taking me into his confidence, asking me how things were going at home, would have offended the integrity of the doctor-patient trust between him and Anna I have no idea. As it was, he declined to say anything more than that he was prepared to see Anna again if she wanted to speak to him before her appointment the following Tuesday. He recommended I encourage her to take hot baths in the meantime to help her relax!

Once again I took Anna home. Inside I was furious with Landis, with what I was sure was his misreading of the situation, its gravity; his refusal to condescend to speak to me, to accept that Anna had broken down, had entered a state of psychosis; and that with two small children at home it was only I, not he, who could keep her and the children intact – or out of a mental hospital.

At home I told Satu that the doctor had said it would 'take a few more days' – it was the only thing I could think of to make the situation sound more hopeful. I could hardly say that Landis hadn't spoken to me at all except to recommend Anna take hot baths and get some sleep.

'It must be very difficult for you,' Satu managed to say in her painfully slow English. But in my diary I noted that it was Anna who needed most consideration, who was suffering most deeply. 'And if I am making up for past years of escape – well, that is as it should be.'

Landis's apparent lack of concern had in fact strengthened my own determination not to fail Anna. It had become, for the first time at a conscious level, a matter of honour. I wanted Anna to get better: but I was going to prove to her that this didn't mean rejection and incarceration in an asylum to force her to behave as a dutiful wife. It was a mortal decision: but I took it out of love and as a sincere duty, something I had never been able to do before in all the years that we had known each other. However threatening it was to the existing framework of our lives, I felt that the time had come to act, to open ourselves to the future – a better future for Anna, who had supported me emotionally and domestically for eight years. The implication that most of all it was I who must change – that I must begin to review my own life and what I was doing to Anna – that only came later as the situation darkened and any notion of a quick 'recovery' was washed away. In those early days of the breakdown I saw only Anna's suffering, the apparent unconcern of her psychiatrist, and thus my own obligation to support her – an obligation strengthened by the years I had spent on my biography and its themes of courage and moral growth.

10

Anna had now stopped talking to me, as she had stopped talking to Landis. Though I ran her a hot bath when we got home she didn't sleep that night; and the next day, Friday, she began to go on all fours, even in the garden, sometimes making low cries of distress and moans of anguish. She seemed to be withdrawing into an ever deeper, more suffering self, perhaps into childhood, her memory of loss, of war, of flight, of orphanages, tanks, of near-starvation and unending lack of hope, of human warmth. Little Thomas, who had been so dear to her – who had been raised with such confidence and intelligence, such humour and guiltless love – he couldn't understand what was happening and would shriek with fear if Anna came near him now, and clung to me.

'Went for a long, long walk in the park,' I noted in my diary. 'Fed the deer and ducks. Anna chain-smoking, not speaking to me at all. In the afternoon Satu took Thomas out and fetched Gabriel, who played then with a friend till 6. I actually slept upstairs – Anna lying awake the whole time beside me, as though drugged. (I had given her one Mogadon to encourage her to sleep, but it seemed not to have the slightest effect.) Made children their supper, put them to bed. Watched T.V. for an hour. A. actually doing one or two things for the children – fetching things, for example, which bode a little better. When I went up to bed, though, at 12 p.m. she was still awake, lying in Gabriel's bed – Gabriel in mine. Went to sleep, woken at 1.30 a.m. by sound of Anna's cries – throaty, choking screeches. Curiously

Thomas slept through it all. Tried to calm her down. I asked if she had slept. She said yes, but it seemed unlikely.'

Relatively speaking it was a calm day that Friday; and if Anna got no rest, at least I had some sleep: an essential factor if we were going to survive this period – particularly the children and Satu. Saturday, however, was different.

11

By Saturday evening I was having second thoughts about the whole venture: 'Tired, uncertain about it all. Gabriel wetting his bed even before going to sleep – is it fair on them? The look on Joe's [Gabriel's friend] face when Anna started to roll in the dirt outside, groaning, then drawing up her legs, head bent down like Mohammedans at worship. Being sick on her dress, incontinent even this evening . . . oh, where can it lead to? Or why does it have to be?

'Yesterday seems so long ago I can hardly bring it to mind . . . A. still not having slept I fear, despite the Mogadon.

'It occurs to me – supposing she is going permanently insane? But on second thoughts this no longer exists.

'At 8.30 this morning A. already down. Can she have slept at all? It seems impossible that she can even *survive* physically without sleep for so long. Got her to take bath – her underclothes stained with blood and smears of it hanging from her in the bath. Seems no better, if anything, worse. I fetched more fags, meanwhile she put on a black coat which she kept on throughout the day. Was sick in the garden. I rang Landis at lunchtime – asked if he realized how serious A.'s condition was. He offered help – said A. had asked that it should be this way, that she had not had chance to work out her breakdowns on previous occasions. But it isn't help I need – it's encouragement! And no one seems to have consulted me – discussed between L. + A. beforehand, but without saying anything to me – unless A.'s attempt to get me to read Cooper and Laing be called that.'

I remember my sinking feeling while talking to Landis, and my anger. I asked how Anna could possibly be said to be responsible for any decisions, such as whether to continue at home like this, when she was so patently *not* in control of herself, her mind or her actions. Landis was silent at first, and then replied that no one could say what was going on inside Anna, but that he had seen her original letter to Laing saying that she didn't wish to be hospitalized if she broke down again, but wanted a chance to come through herself . . .

'In the afternoon Joe there. But how to shield the children from A.'s state? When she grovels in the dust and dirt or begins to screech hysterically, twist round and round the staircase post until she collapses on the ground: Oh, Christ, there are other ways in which we torture kids without being aware of it: but they cannot be so tragic as this.

'Where will it end? I give A. a bath again after the children are in bed, and when I stare at her intently she actually speaks to me: "Why are you staring at me like that, David Reed?" – almost the first words she has spoken to me directly since Wednesday.

'Obviously, stopping the pill has resulted in a haemorrhage, her underclothes again are stained and I soak them, as well as disinfecting the carpet where she has peed in the bedroom. Her skin, after the bath, curiously soft again – and despite the disfiguration of the "illness" ("she has lots of different faces," Gabriel remarks, "lots of frightening faces," and he shows me some of them – one the idiot's stare with mouth open), her face is still . . . pretty.

'My fear? That I shall prove too weak, that I cannot face the prospect – or presence – of an invalid, it is such a restriction on my own freedom.

'But what is freedom? I had the choice years ago, when I could have said no. Now it no longer exists – for how would I ever look myself in the eye if I left her when she is so patently helpless – not only without me, but without someone to care for her?'

I no longer have the letter I wrote to my friend, James Preston, who had gone up to Scotland on holiday. He didn't keep it; but it was the only long letter I sent during this period, and I remember writing it. I was at last beginning to probe my feelings and fears, attempting to define what I was doing, what was really at risk. What had begun as something *faute de mieux*, while I was waiting for Landis to wake up, was now taking a much deeper significance for my own life. Slowly something was cutting into me – and perhaps I was angry at Landis for forcing me to know this. My weary, somewhat brittle determination began to link up with something deeper: this act of outward love began to feel its root in a more profound soil – some area of me that I had been trying to keep under for twenty-nine years.

12

In snatches over the past few days and nights I had begun to read at last Laing's *The Divided Self*. I felt guilty that I had left it so long; and yet the work on my biography had convinced me that there are certain notions, attitudes and ideas that cannot be confronted prematurely – that is, if you are really going to look. I had previously held aloof from existential and phenomenological psychology because it threatened the order I had been trying to set in my life; also I did not wish to encroach on Anna's own territory. I respected her sensitivity to moral, social, and political issues; I wanted that to be her own, inviolate from me, a field in which she could be proud of her own insights and perceptions, and not feel that I had taken over. I didn't realize that it was my understanding that she wanted, nothing more.

The book had a profound effect on me. Much of it, for such a well-known and well-quoted work, was technical and remote: but in the context of what was happening here in my own life almost every word had relevance and added significance. It was, above all, the reading of *The Divided Self* which turned my patience and dutiful tolerance into probing and discovery. Many events recounted in that book were to be repeated in our own lives.

I read most of that Saturday evening after the children were asleep; and on Sunday I took Anna with them to my twin brother's house.

'The weather was fine, mostly we sat and the children played in the garden. When Stephen first started talking about Scandinavia it was like listening to a traveller in a men's club. My own twin! And when we talk Bridget mentions some of the things her friends say: "don't know how you *manage* financially," or about schools, National Health Service, etc. – which make *me* wonder what world they are living in. Still, they listen, which is something, while I say why I think it is wrong to send one's children to private schools. Anna crawling about on all fours in the garden – yet she ate all her lunch, drank wine, etc., without compunction. It was when I went out into the garden to fetch her for tea that she spoke my name and for the first time in days allowed me to hold her hand. I felt so close then, so sure that love somehow had broken through at last – as I'd felt so often at the mental hospital, but all too late! Eight years to read *The Divided Self*!'

It was a wonderful and salutary day at Stephen's, for it brought far more than just an afternoon's respite for me. Anna's 'illness' was beginning to affect my thinking, and the world was looking different to me. It was the first time since Stephen's marriage that I felt neither envy nor rivalry, the first time since we were at school that I felt him close to me as my brother, my twin. Writing the biography had led up to this with its theme of brotherhood. I remember, towards the end of the manuscript, as the lives of the brothers drew near to their close, I had written to Stephen to tell him of it: and how much our own relationship had been part of it. I suppose I was saying: after our years of separation and competitiveness, I feel I have reached a point of détente – we can start disarming, it's peace. Somehow Anna's distress, the crisis of her 'illness', of our very marriage, provided the context in which to find our way back to each other. So that I wanted to cry afterwards.

For Anna really seemed to have improved that day. 'At home in the evening Anna doing her dancing and hand-gesturing act, so I put on a Greek record – and she danced to it! Seems as though she is rediscovering her body – her embodied self, as Laing calls it. Made supper for her. More! she demanded and I had to give her my own; this greed reminding me of something, perhaps a past occasion – an assertion of her own demands and desires which is good; and so I give her my own, gratefully almost.

'I felt sure then that the main crisis was somehow over – perhaps it was also Laing's remarks about the pretences of schizophrenia – for the best reasons – which confirmed it: all the funny faces Anna made at Stephen's that made me laugh, feel she was putting on a charade really, but not one I resented in the least, now that the terror of it all had begun to subside.'

'Peter rang, and I spoke to him as though it *was* all over,' I noted the following day; 'though this morning I realize there may well be a relapse, or at any rate a slowing down: a disinclination to re-enter the world of responsibilities and demands again. That, at least, is one aspect of NHS hospitals which must encourage patients to leave, namely the discipline and imposed order, the "walls" . . .'

The continuing sentence ends in mid-thought. I must have been utterly exhausted, for the size of the words as well as the spaces between them were increasing. After that the page went blank; and I have no further records until three days later: Thursday, 17 May 1973.

13

Whether I lost the loose diary sheet on which I recorded those intervening days, I don't know. Somehow I doubt if I wrote anything. Gabriel, who was six, still had to be taken to school and collected in the afternoon, Thomas had to be looked after all day; and Anna's condition now got steadily more serious.

I know that on Tuesday, 15 May, I took Anna once again to Landis; and this time too he failed to respond. Once again I went for a walk, and returned to find that she had not spoken; though this time she had at least – at the very end of the session apparently – gone into Landis's consulting-room.

The problem was, however, that she wouldn't leave. The next patient, a boy, came in and sat down; but Anna resolutely declined to go. The boy sat waiting as the precious minutes of his own consultation ticked away, as well as Anna's own life. It was a strange moment, for until now Landis's whole existential approach to therapy had been to wait and see what Anna said or did, and not to initiate anything himself. He was playing a waiting game; and Anna had played his game back at him.

Now he had two patients in the same room. He could, I suppose, have kept Anna there; but he looked embarrassed and appealed to me to intervene, repeating time and again that Anna's session was over, and that it wasn't fair on the next patient. It was almost laughable. It seemed to contradict the very ethos of the therapy – and reminded me of the similar incongruence of payment for psychiatry.

I took Anna away. At home she moved into a period of spasms, in which her whole body would go rigid. She began to somersault, to contort her body in strange exercises, as though tightening herself into some kind of mechanical desensitized object or motor, in which she might escape – thudding into furniture and bruising herself quite horribly so that I had to restrain her. She didn't notice. It was as though something were petrifying inside her; and again I was frightened.

14

Anna had still, to the best of my knowledge, not slept a single hour since the day her breakdown began. I had rarely slept more than a few hours each night. That Wednesday – 16 May – I fell asleep at midnight. At 3 there was a loud rapping at the front door which woke me. I went downstairs in my pyjamas. There were two uniformed policemen there.

'Are you Mr Reed?'

'Yes.'

'We've a Mrs Reed at the police station saying she has murdered her children.'

I stood stunned.

'We don't imagine she means it, but we'd like to check. Which room do the children sleep in?'

I led them upstairs. Everything was peaceful in the children's room. They were breathing quietly and regularly. I put some clothes on and went down to the station in the car they had brought. The duty-sergeant said that he'd called an ambulance in case I wanted it; or should he send it away? I told him to send it away.

Anna was sitting in a bare little room with a policewoman. She wouldn't speak to me, but clearly she recognized me. The sergeant offered to have us driven home, but I said we'd prefer to walk.

As we went up the hill I realized that Anna was wearing no shoes. Once before, perhaps only days before her breakdown, Landis later told me, Anna had telephoned him late at night and announced that she had killed the children. But even if she hadn't actually touched them, the statement to the police was obviously symbolic, and a warning. For some time I had sensed that, asleep, I was running the risk that Anna might choose to take a knife to me – I had, after all, deprived her of her illusory 'child', the one she wanted; and over the years I had violated her by caging her, having sex with her. I recognized latent violence in the situation; yet strangely I had no fear – partly because I was convinced that I loved her, utterly and completely.

But here the threat was to the children themselves, and that worried me. Everything inside me told me that the children had to go through this with us. This experience had to be theirs too, so that they would never feel puzzled by Anna's inability to cope. They would come to feel for her, to recognize their stake in her struggle. And amazingly, they *had* already grown to accept and not be too frightened of the situation. What if Anna was now warning me?

In the morning – for I was too shaken to sleep again – we walked in the park. There was a blustering wind that blew through the chestnuts and over the grass. It was cold. Anna began talking in a sort of delirium, as though in a dream, her voice desolate. The night before I had got her to watch a play on the television; and after that the news.

'Stephen's message,' Anna kept repeating; and when I asked her what she meant, she explained that it had been Stephen speaking after the play: to tell us, to warn me.

'We are the last. We are the bones. Dead.'

Such had been the message. An aeroplane flew overhead. 'The last,' Anna commented. Dogs being walked in the park struck a sort of terror into her, as though they were trackers, intent on catching us.

It was difficult to get her to say more, as it had been since the beginning. But now there was something else too, which was reflected in the physical contortions she went through: an enormous desolation, a profound conviction – the certainty – that a great catastrophe had taken place, that the world had been devastated. It was as though World War III had been fought: and we were the lone survivors.

What lay behind her symbolic confession at the police station I didn't then know. But I took her with me to see Landis knowing that this time something *must* be done, that he must wake up to her condition and her suffering.

15

We arrived early. 'Landis appeared eventually in anorak. Anna says nothing. Landis makes tea. How long can this charade of "manageable silence" go on, I wonder.

'At last I say: "Do you want to tell Roy where we were at 3 a.m. this morning?" Have to say it myself in the end. Anna licking her lips constantly, manically, smoking heavily still, smoking the fag-ends right up against metal screws on chair. Runs out and up the road. Stands on sink to see if window will open (we are on the fourth floor). Eventually Roy agrees to arrange help.'

It had taken all this to move Landis. Yet I suppose that this was Landis's point – though he never explained it: that if we were to come through madness it was no use panicking or pressing Anna in any direction except the one that she felt she must go in.

That day, in the kitchen at Landis's, with a cold sun shining and Anna somersaulting into the cupboards like a thudding brick, standing on the sink unit, running downstairs and away: it seemed so obviously an appeal, a 'performance' designed to show Landis what was happening to her, how terrible it was – not consciously such, yet to me unmistakable. When Landis finally said we must do something, Anna's whole behaviour altered. She sat on the floor at our feet, on the coarse cord carpet, as Landis went through the alternatives.

First, he could try to get people down to help us through this crisis period; secondly, we could try to get Anna into a nursing home. There was also the third possibility of Anna entering his 'community'. He asked Anna which she would prefer.

Anna wouldn't answer, if indeed she heard the question. She smoked as though the world was about to end, hysterically, her eyes wild and fearful. Landis put another question. Would she like him or me to decide?

For a response she put out her hands and held us both by the legs, as though to say: I trust you both. Both of you will look after me. I'll not choose between you.

'So David will make the decision,' Landis said to her when it became obvious she wouldn't speak.

I looked at Anna, and at Landis. I don't know what nursing home I could have chosen; I had no medical insurance and the National Health Service was unlikely to help other than by hospitalizing her and giving electroconvulsive treatment. It meant therefore finding a private home. Or else there was the 'community', about which I knew next to nothing, except that it was a place where people 'freaked out' – but which Anna had never seen. Or there was our house, where Anna was in her own surroundings, with her own children present, not banished. I felt that if only Landis would support me instead of playing Buddha in his room, if he would come over to our house, if he had colleagues and helpers who could help me to help Anna ...

I therefore chose that.

Whether I was right or wrong I don't know. I don't suppose I shall ever know. The question of National Health hospitalization wasn't even mentioned. I felt: if things get worse, if I cannot cope, we can always keep these other options open.

Landis promised to phone me that night to tell me who would be coming to help, and when. He himself would also, from now on, come to us.

I took Anna home. 'In car rigor again, contorting violently.' She kept moving into the neighbour's garden and scaling his wall to the street after we arrived. The au pair went out, and to keep Anna in the house while I bathed the children I locked the back door.

Suddenly there was a crash and the sound of splintering glass.

A hole had appeared in the kitchen window, and an empty wine bottle lay on the floor where it had fallen back. After that I didn't lock any doors.

Landis rang eventually just before midnight. A girl called Patty would come the following day, a helper at the community; and perhaps there'd be others. I felt relieved, especially at the thought that I might get some sleep from now on, and that there would be other people to reduce the risk of an accident or injury. I wondered what sort of person Patty would be.

16

Patty came for an hour only, the following day. It was Friday, 18 May 1973. She said she couldn't stay but would return the next day. She was American, tall and broad-built, like a life-size Russian doll. I never did find an English helper.

The next morning she brought a week-end bag and a companion with her, another big girl: Gunhilda, a German with short hair, spectacles, and a very deep voice. They squeezed past, balloonlike, nurses of the spirit. A part of me, I know, had longed for help, for support: yet, now that it was here, I felt strangely hostile, welcoming them, yet in my heart resenting the intrusion – above all, resenting the fact that I needed help from such strangers.

Patty stayed the night, sleeping downstairs on the settee. I gave

Anna two sleeping tablets, and while she slept for a few hours in the late evening I talked to Patty.

She said she thought the situation impossible for one person to cope with. She'd seen the children, seen how much I needed to give them in order to make sure they didn't suffer; she said she was amazed I'd managed to keep the home going for so long, but that in the end it would harm the children and wouldn't actually 'help' Anna. She could see the terror in Anna's eyes, her hostility too: she felt that Anna needed to be able to get away from this situation, to get away from her responsibilities towards the children – responsibilities she couldn't fulfil – that she needed peace and isolation in order to confront her own condition.

Should I have listened?

I was disturbed by Patty's views. They negated what I had been trying to do over the past fortnight. Worse, they seemed to exclude me, as Landis did – as though I were irrelevant to Anna's basic problems. Or at least they implied that Anna needed to get away from me, from our marriage, in order to live out this madness. I suppose my pride was injured. But how could I 'hand over' Anna to these helpers, any more than I could hand her over for National Health shock treatment? I felt such a profound conviction that most of all Anna needed love – total, dedicated love, the love that had been removed with the death of her father in the war, and that her mother, in the war's aftermath, had simply not been able to provide. I needed to prove that love both to her and to myself – prove to her that I would go all the way through madness with her and still love her at the end; never take the children away or reject her. Patty's attitude seemed to ignore all this. It seemed cautious and frightened, and to reflect Patty's own rather middle-class home background in America rather than our own situation.

Landis had phoned and asked whether, when he came the next day, Sunday, he could bring R. D. Laing as consultant. I was surprised and hesitant: and Landis asked what was the matter. I wasn't sure why I reacted that way. I suppose, now, that it was difficult for me to adjust suddenly to these attentions paid after two weeks of neglect, and that I felt suspicious about too many people coming to gape.

Talking to Patty that Saturday night, I determined to talk over with Laing the pros and cons of home 'treatment'. Patty confessed that her only experience had been in the States with schizophrenics who were taken out of their home environment and treated in a hostel – young people who needed above all to be released from the schizophrenic pressures of their family. Patty had been there a year. She had only recently arrived in England, and her only experience here had been at the 'community'.

We took it in turns to stay awake, in case Anna needed attention or tried to run away. At one stage, while Patty was supposed to be awake, Anna tiptoed to the front door, opened it, and began to walk down the road after a neighbour who was going to work early. Someone in the street saw her and brought her back.

This quiet leaving of the house was to be habitual in the coming weeks. I never really knew what was signified: whether Patty was right, that Anna needed to be taken out of her home responsibilities, or whether it was simply a desire to act out impulses that came over her – the impulse to go out and seek something, or the feeling that she was being driven away and was testing me.

I went to sleep wondering what Laing would make of it all.

17

Landis and Laing arrived at about a quarter to twelve the next morning. It was a brilliantly sunny spring day and I had taken the children out on bicycle and toy tractor round the block. I saw the black taxi standing outside the house. Landis and Laing had their backs to me and were discussing loudly whether it was worth asking the taxi to wait, or to come back in an hour; or whether they should order a fresh one. Laing was wearing a velvet jacket with smart, casual trousers. I introduced myself and the children.

'I gather you've been going through a difficult time,' Laing said as he shook my hand. His Scottish accent was more pronounced than I remembered from the television interview I had once seen; he seemed to have rings of suffering round his eyes rather than lines on his forehead.

When I took them into the house Anna appeared at the top of the stairs, and then disappeared again. Laing went straight up after her – I liked him for that, for that immediate reaction. Landis went through into the sitting-room to talk to Patty.

A friend came to take the children off for a walk in the park, and I made coffee for everyone. I took it upstairs, where by now Anna, Laing, Landis, and Patty had congregated in our bedroom. After a few moments Anna went out. Laing was sitting, leisurely sprawled, on the bed while Landis and Patty sat on the carpet by the windows. I began to put my questions.

They stayed probably little more than an hour; yet Laing's directness was of great importance after Landis's refusal to include me. I asked Laing whether Anna ought to go away as Patty felt; or whether I myself should take her away from home and the children, who might be reminding her of responsibilities she couldn't fulfil. Laing said no – at least as things then stood.

'It seems to me she relates to all this,' he said, motioning at the books and pictures around the room. 'Everything is very expressive of her.'

It was the first time that I had been aware of how much the house reflected Anna – its sombre colours, the walls of books, the magazine photographs of gypsies, of Mexicans, of starving children pinned up. Laing added: 'though I expect she can also be a very tidy person' – and that was also true: at times she had actually seemed to clean me out of the house, gathering my books, letters, and oddments in boxes and putting them in the hall for me to take away to my study.

But what of her condition?

Again Laing spoke out without casting the question back at me as Landis had done on the one occasion I had phoned him. Laing seemed to feel that perhaps the worst was over, that the psychosis wouldn't last very long now – 'though she can always have it shocked back into her in a matter of a day or two,' he pointed out, 'if ECT is used. But it will only be back inside.'

Landis told me afterwards that he'd disagreed with Laing's

prognosis about the length of time it would take Anna to emerge from her psychosis, that he felt that there was a great deal more that must be worked through before she was clear. For the moment, however, he said nothing.

Above all, I asked, was it possible for me to know whether I were a hindrance or help to Anna in working through this trial? To look after her at home meant always to look at her with eyes that wanted her to come back, for I loved her – and perhaps this made it worse for Anna.

Laing's response was without hesitation. He repeated my phrase. 'That, David, is exactly what she needs. We all want that.'

The two left in the taxi which had brought them, and in the afternoon I took Anna and the children to my brother's house for tea. Patty went home, apparently surprised that Laing should have seen the situation as he did, but deeply respectful.

However, Laing had said one thing which I didn't note in my diary at the time but have not forgotten. In his emphatic Scottish accent he added to his prognosis: 'But don't let's lose our common sense,' pointing out that the situation could at any time alter and require different decisions.

It was a sort of warning. Apart from an accidental meeting outside an Underground station three weeks later, I never saw him again.

18

At my brother's house Anna remained silent, but, as my diary notes, 'apart from hiding under table, no disasters'. Gabriel's attention was entirely taken by a tree-house and by his aunt feeding the baby.

We came home after the children had been bathed. I put them to bed. At 9.30 Patty's companion of the previous day arrived; then my friend Peter; and at 10.30, Sarah, the woman who managed my shop, who had come to announce that she wanted to leave. Anna cowered silently in the corner of the kitchen where we were eating, seating herself symbolically in the waste-bin; then she began a 'quiet torrent of self-effacement and abuse – "trampled in the dirt, fucked silly"' – and in a strange session with Gunhilda, the German girl, they continued this until about three in the morning, when Anna finally came upstairs.

She was excited, and much too lively to sleep. We just lay there for an hour. Then suddenly she seemed to go rigid, leaning forward as though to somersault: the prelude to a terrifying twelve hours – 'as tense, as seized, as "possessed" as witches in the Middle Ages', was how I described it in my diary afterwards. At 7.30 a.m. I gave her a bath, with Thomas helping me as he had also woken by then. I left the room for thirty seconds with Thomas when there was a tremendous crash. I ran up: Anna was standing by the louvred window holding two quarter-inch panes she had smashed and then wrenched out. She seemed poised, intent on hurling herself out of the hole she had made – 'virtually uncontrollable – self-destruction in her eyes. Gunhilda helps, but v. frightened inside I see. Anna goes over to next-door neighbour in morning while I have an hour's sleep. Gunhilda leaves. In afternoon I take Anna to friend's flat – there she tries to leap out of imaginary window in kitchen ceiling, throwing herself up and falling flat on her back – thought her arm was broken. Return home – there got her on toilet (she had wet herself at friend's) – and with great sighs she relieves her constipation – and as if it were a flood receding, the whole spasm just ebbs away in minutes. Sleeps whole night without tablets.'

19

'Wake at 5 a.m. Quiet day after Gabriel to school. Play with Thomas.

'Anna still completely deluded though – tidies room and changes into trousers, arranges newspapers, but otherwise lost and signs of almost complete amnesia. "The bombs dropped in the corner," pointing to the corner of the room. "We're all dead."

Occasionally still: "Too late." "*Pferdegans* [fat goose]" while pulling her hair. And "I smell".'

She was evidently nowhere near recovery. She talked constantly of the 'CIA' conspiracy; yet for the moment she was physically calm. Then at 5 p.m. Patty came, and Anna showed signs of physical nerves again – slipped under the table after supper and moved into 'launching position' in garden, whispering she is a horse when I ask her, and pointing to patches on her knees (reminder of breeches I suppose).

'Make children's supper, but I know my patience has reached end. I need *sleep*.

'Went to bed, but as I was falling asleep – that feeling of being in a far-off room, sinking or rather slipping into a phantasy world – was woken by Thomas screaming – had had a quarrel with Gabriel. Took him into my bed, but he seemed so terribly over-excited, nervous, that I felt ready to break down, to shatter I was so exhausted and angry. Picked him up and put him into his own bed (Gabriel already asleep) and read him his sailor book, smiling and beginning to calm down. Smiling and looking into my face – he'd got what he wanted. Brought him a bottle, and he went to sleep straight away. Passed out myself shortly afterwards, having coaxed Anna to bed with me and given her two sleeping tablets.'

20

Tuesday, 22 May 1973

'Woke at 3 a.m. – Anna wanting to get up and only restrained by my pleas. She had not wanted her nightgown when we first went to sleep, and was relatively willing to be touched – might be a good sign, sign of greater awareness of own body even if self-destructive still and unhappy. At 3.45 a.m. she went downstairs. Patty said she ran out and over neighbour's fence "down the block". Patty fetched her back then, having told me.

'Knock on the door at 7.30 a.m. Roy Landis. I got up and

shaved. Anna had still not spoken to him, but seemed "very peaceful" as Patty put it. Roy stayed till 12.'

'Smelling – sniffing always – "I smell" (of a horse?).

'"I'm burned out."

'"Where shall I go?"

'"The family stuff is burnt out" (fingering the patches on the knees of her jeans).

'I ask her if she wants to run away? Whether we should go for a walk?

'"Uh – hurgh. They've got the lanes ready."

'"The lanes?" I query.

'"The pig lanes."

'"For slaughter?" I ask, guessing.

'"Yes."

'"Do you feel you're a pig?"

'"A pig and a dog."'

Then she herself began a question: 'Why didn't Patty ... nobody could stop me.'

'What?' I asked her when she said no more.

'Setting fire to the whole world.'

It is difficult to describe what it was like: and to everyone the situation appeared different, according to their own conception. That day a painter friend came round, who was eighty-two, asking just to see Anna. She had never been in our house before. 'Will you show me round?' she asked Anna: and Anna took her by the hand and showed her the entire house, the garden, even her own study up the steps. 'No one understands,' she said to her at one stage.

Yet that same afternoon Anna ran away while I sat jotting some notes in my diary; and I had to alert the police to find her.

And why? Each time Anna wandered out I had to ask myself this question: whether to feel concern, responsibility, or whether to accept Anna's right to experience, to live through this mental turbulence in her own way, without being too closely watched, guarded.

It was true, though, that no hospital would give Anna the

freedom she had at home: she would always be a patient; and I felt simply that the penalty of being at home as against the greater strictness of hospital as an asylum was that I couldn't let her run away on her own, that I was responsible for her safety and that I would never forgive myself – or be forgiven – if I didn't look after her.

Fortunately I found her a few hours later, not a hundred yards from the house. A neighbour had seen her. She was standing on the pavement watching the comings and goings of lorries at a haulage contractor's. She seemed bewildered by the traffic around our own house when I brought her home.

'They don't know the right direction,' she cried. 'They're lost.'

This statement of Anna's pointed up the difference between my own and the community helpers' attitude to Anna's madness. Patty felt – and from a phenomenological point of view this seemed quite reasonable – that those cars *were* directionless in a meaningful sense, were lost. Why *were* they going so fast? Home? But what was a home that made you drive so urgently, manically? There was thus – as Laing was at pains to point out in other cases – a sanity-within-insanity, perhaps a higher sanity in what Anna said.

But to me this interpretation seemed naïve – irritatingly so. While wishing to feel with Anna as best I could, I felt it vitally important *not* to go too far: we had to preserve our own common sense and sanity lest we actually encourage Anna on a course that, if it went on too long, could only end in disaster, for her or for us. However she behaved, *we* had to preserve a practical, everyday world to which she *could* one day return and in which she would be able to cope with the oppressions of noise, etc.: a world she could respect however much she might temporarily reject it. Somehow it seemed ridiculous to treat Anna as some kind of guru or prophet when she was in such obvious distress. In doing so we would actually be abdicating our responsibility towards her by giving *her* the lead – and thus isolating her even more. Every intuition told me that we must show the deepest compassion we could find in ourselves. Her struggle was fundamentally with her self; it was not a social phenomenon.

She should be encouraged to feel there *was* a real world she could return to, and which loved her.

This fundamental difference was to underlie our attitudes right to the end.

That night, though apparently very tired, Anna couldn't sleep at all. She took exception to yet another 'helper' sent by Landis: Dan, a shy, gangly eighteen-year-old. He arrived at 6.30. When we ate supper Anna took her food off the table and ate it with her back to us, as though to protest at the way I was bringing in strangers. When I tried to get her to rest she kept reappearing in the kitchen as I talked with the American boy, complaining at the 'noises'. At 5.30 next morning she still hadn't slept – and ran out of the house. Dan brought her back; and I went for a walk with her. 'Still speaks of the world being dead. Wanted me to take her "over to the other side" – before it "rained".

'When I asked what would happen if we didn't get there in time, she muttered about milk bottles exploding. As we walked on I realized her preoccupation with milk sounds must be because of the dairy unloading their crates which had kept her awake last night. (Also the pub very noisy at midnight)'.

Sixteen days of insanity, of psychosis, had passed.

'Was the girl at the museum who showed me the Tsar Peter the Great Exhibition Elizabeth or Christine?' she asked me at the haulage contractor's. I said that I didn't know who she was.

'"His daughter."

'"Whose?"

'"The Tsar's!"'

And at another time: 'Mrs Audrey (the old painter) – she's your grandmother.' Yet such remarks were too related to specific events and people to be insignificant, and too significant in their implications to be random. Which came first? Were the things she spoke of (or their symbolisms) the origin of her condition – or was her own anguish and distress merely bound to express itself in a hypersensitivity to the distress and threats implicit in the world about us?

21

'It's too late,' Anna kept repeating – though more of a question than a statement. 'Where shall I go?' she was asking as she paced the bedroom.

It was early in the morning on Thursday, 24 May 1973. Anna slept a little then from 6-ish to 8 a.m. I took Gabriel to school. At 10.30 a tidal flood warning siren went off, a quite frightening sound in the circumstances. We jumped into the car and drove to the shop, where a policeman told us it was only a test.

'Relieved – but still agitated – drove up to James Preston's house. Miranda gave Anna a massage. Went for a walk in the park with their dog.

'"That was your mother," Anna insisted about her several times.

'"That was Mrs Audrey." (For Miranda?)

'"Maintains I'm blind."

'"When did Satu come along?"'

It was weird, like being with someone from another planet, out of science-fiction.

22

Friday

'Took Anna and Thomas to country – brilliant sunshine – visited Lullingstone Park, a golf course on a series of green hills that seemed to stretch for miles. Anna wanting to return to a little grocery shop where we'd bought ice-cream. When we walked through a wood to the second tee Anna disappears. Leave Thomas playing in a sand bunker and chase around asking people if they've seen her. Eventually find her wandering at bottom of hill to one side of the course; but in the meantime Thomas, upset, has been looking for me and wandered about ¼ mile back to car. I run after him, calling his name. He turns, unaware of where the voice comes from, sees me, and runs towards me as fast as his little legs will propel him. Like a film. I can see from his purple eyes he has been crying.

'"You're not safe today," says one golfer, who is taking precautions by standing behind a tree; "they're all beginners."'

I took them then to the old village of Eynsham, where we picnicked by the river. Thomas paddled and tried to catch fish.

'Return home to late lunch at 3 p.m. When Gabriel comes home from school he sees the little fishing nets I'd bought for their holiday and wants immediately to go to the park – and we do, as Stephen has phoned to say he can't make Friday evening to take the children on half-term holiday as planned. With Anna we march up the road to the park. I say march, for Thomas seems a different child: blossoms suddenly with Gabriel there – puts fishing-net cane between his legs and pretends it's his cock-horse, or on his shoulder in the fashion of a gun and sings left-right, left-right . . .

'At the pond Gabriel learns to catch minnows, while Thomas flails at the water industriously but to no purpose other than catching weeds. Gabriel very excited and proud of his catch. Sound of the traffic rising to insane pitch – everyone leaving on holiday.

'Came home again – Gabriel reluctantly – with our catch.' Patty arrived, and I drove into town to the Aldwych, where I had tickets for Dostoyevsky's *The Possessed*, performed by a Polish ensemble. 'Sell my spare ticket at last moment; then Peter appears unexpectedly out of near-by row – extraordinary coincidence as I'd tried to phone him at 6.30 to offer him the ticket. He'd come "on spec" to theatre at that exact time and bought one.

'Afterwards we have coffee together in the Strand. Peter says he has had feeling that Anna's "normal" state, in a sense, a microcosm of her present condition – a notion which makes R.L.'s remark about "What is normality?" seem less banal. My own feeling is that somehow we – I – ought to treat people like this with more deference and respect for their problems, however "condescending" or conscious that might be: that one *has* to make an effort . . .

54

'Also very resentful about Sonia, Peter's wife, who has never come to see Anna – about friends in general, I suppose,' I added.

It had been a long day: but when I got home at about 1 a.m. Anna was still up. Patty said she had been waiting on the stairs for me, getting up every time there was the sound of a voice outside.

'Overjoyed to see me,' I recorded in my diary.

It was the first time that Anna had shown such a reaction: and when I took her quietly up to bed she slept soundly till 7 a.m.

'Gabriel wakes – all excited about leaving. Stephen arrives finally at 10 a.m.

'Off they go – Gabriel so excited, and even Thomas sitting coyly and quietly in back with Satu.

'Emptiness after they have gone. Cannot get Anna out all day – Patty stays and we chat in the morning.

'"Oh shut up!" Anna says as I start to talk about our area.'

Stephen had offered to take the children (and Satu) for the week of half-term to the country. It seemed to be a natural, logical break for them, a holiday. Above all it promised to relieve Anna. But it didn't. Unless rape be called that.

23

On Sunday I entered in my journal: 'Stay indoors almost entire day – very tiring and claustrophobic. Roy Landis comes at 9 a.m. and stays till 3 p.m.; Anna won't speak to him, but gets very angry when Roy and I talk, so I go to my study for an hour to do some work.

'When Roy gets up to go, Anna mortified – and remains so entire day. She goes to bed early while I type out article.'

24

Monday, Bank Holiday

'Miranda rings and we go up to their house for morning. Stay for lunch on roof. During entire time Anna says nothing. Miranda gives her a bath and washes her hair. Curious how Anna eats quite well and *looks* so well on all this madness! – although the eyes seem to sink deeper each day into their sockets.

'She seems capable now of reading – though only in a fleeting, tangential way. I finish typing and ask if she wants to go to cinema. She nods, so we have supper and drive into town. But in cinema expected happens – first frightened by newsreel, then wanting to leave when film begins. Persuade her to stay twice, but she makes all the motions of being held against her will ("out" she keeps whispering). In the foyer she says: "But it was attacking your parents!" – and though I resent all the waste of time and annoyance of having to leave the film (*The Discreet Charm of the Bourgeoisie* by Buñuel), there is really a great deal of truth in her remark!

'Come home. Walk over to Fair and back (it is closed by 11.30). Cold. Anna holding off from me. She does not come to bed and as far as I know she does not sleep.'

25

Tuesday, 29 May 1973

'Anna appears not to have slept – I don't get up till 9.15 though – a sign of unwillingness to face the present?

'Go with Anna down to library – she stands whole time in corner.

'Make lunch, which Anna eats – otherwise she either sits mute or wanders about the house. After lunch wrote two letters, then began to read. Anna had felt the bones of my hand and said: "But how are you here?"

'"Why should I not be?"'
'"But the Chinese have come!"'
'"How do you make that out?"'
'"The telephone call . . ."'
'Later made tea and toast. Then at 5.30 A. slips out of front door. Migraine coming on, check all round, but too late, she has disappeared.'

26

What I did not enter in the diary was that a part of me actually *wanted* Anna to run away that day. I was simply reaching the end of my spiritual resources; I had no help, and the weeks of rejection by Anna, the seeming endlessness of the psychosis conspired to make me long inside for a solution, whatever it might be. I don't think it was mere coincidence I suffered a migraine that day. Something had to break. But whether it was Anna's hypersensitivity to this atmosphere which drove her to run out I don't know, will never know. She had run away before. But this time it was different. Though we alerted the police and scoured the whole neighbourhood she proved impossible to find that night. It poured and poured, but she didn't come home.

27

Wednesday, 30 May 1973
'Sleep again. Wake at 8-ish. Phone police, no sign. Then at 9.30 a.m. they phone to say she is there. Nip down in van. She is with James's wife Miranda (and 3 dogs) looking quite *beaming*, blooming – and though I have brought socks, shoes, and coat her trousers hardly feel wet and her jersey is quite dry. Put her into the bath I had to leave – where *she* promptly washes herself completely and vigorously with soap, utterly calm. Feel very tired,

migraine aftermath, get A. some pyjamas and we go to bed – even sleep, though Anna does not look, curiously, in the least tired. Wake about 11, telephone ringing. Peter, who says will come over. Comes at 12. Talks about his father, his depression over the week-end, his love-making with D. – working off resentments, which she seems to understand. Though Peter sees me as having solved the problem he has failed with (father), I all too clearly see the ways I have *not* "solved" it; or rather the penalties exacted for having solved it – falling into the same trap as my father, etc. Anna appears several times at door but shies back.

'Make lunch, chops, and in afternoon go for walk in park. Anna says nothing so far, wearing green pullover and narrow-ankled jeans with patches. Peter leaves at 5 p.m. and we sit in kitchen for a cup of tea. I ask again about last night.

'Suddenly Anna tells it all – very matter of fact:

'"You told me to leave," she says – and when I ask how she gives motion of the head.

'"And where did you spend the night?"

'"At the Fair."

'"But not sleeping on the ground?"

'"No, two boys took me into their caravan."

'"How old were these boys?"

'"Boys."

'"But how old?"

'"Twenty."

'"And they let you sleep in their caravan?"

'"Yes."

'"And did they sleep with you?"

'"Yes."

'"I mean . . . did they . . . ?"

'"They rubbed me up."

'"Rubbed you up?"

'"They fucked me."

'I was flabbergasted by this. My whole body trembled, and I could hear my heart beating. So that was why she looked so remarkably unaffected by the night out in the rain!

'"Are you quite sure they . . . had sex with you? Did they put their penises in? Both of them?"

'"Yes." Anna motions with her hands to indicate their changing places.

'"How many times?"

'She shrugs. "I had a deep dream." That she had gone into fire and water – but in the meantime the prospect of her getting pregnant by two fairground louts – quite apart from all the sexual feelings it evokes in me (I find I am erect) – alarms me almost to hysteria.

'"But suppose they've made you pregnant?"

'She shakes her head – still as cool as a cucumber. "They couldn't have."

'"Why not?"

'"They blew gas into me."

'"Blew gas into you?"

'"Out of the end of their penises. Anyway they were only made of rubber."

'"You mean they wore contraceptives?"

'She shakes her head.

'"Their penises were made of rubber."

'This all explains an earlier reference in the day to a broadcast my younger brother Martin is supposed to have made "on the radio under the bed", to the effect that today Anna must die. She looks triumphant that she hasn't, though by this time – probably sensing my confusion and alarm – she starts to make for the door again, saying "they" are coming for her, that she has to go.

'Dan arrives. I try to question Anna further (Dan starts telling me of the wonders of Rome, not the most appropriate moment).

'I feel terrible – savage with sexual envy, of wounded pride, wanting to beat Anna, feeling as though I am nothing, humiliated and revealed as nobody to Anna after all these weeks of stamina and, yes, courage. All too clearly I see the *positive* side – the liberation implied; but underneath I cannot stop myself seething.

'Go and see our G P. Gives me oestrogen tablets for Anna to induce immediate haemorrhage. I feel quite violent. Talk to Dan about it over supper – cold ham on bread and salad. Our roles reverse, he becomes the psychiatrist, forcing me to face up to the truth of the situation. But underneath I don't wish to!

'Go and see James and Miranda – M. gives me head massage.

We talk about it very openly – both James and Miranda feel it to be a positive sign.

'Return at 12 – Anna quite restless now – had talked of "torture" to Dan apparently, the torture of telling people different stories. Go to bed, but Anna lies on the floor, not sharing the bed – memories of night before?

'In middle of night I hear noise of door, go outside. Two police cars there, Anna and Dan standing with two officers. I say Anna is my wife.

'"Well take her home, Chief, take her home," says the fatter one quite angrily.'

28

In law – assuming Anna's story were true and somehow it seemed too real not to be – the two boys were guilty of rape in taking advantage of a woman not in her senses. Yet I wasn't concerned with 'revenge'. Besides, keeping Anna at home with me, as opposed to hospitalizing her, was a denial that she *was* 'out' of her senses. My action implied that everything she said and experienced at this time – however insane in the average, worldly sense – was significant to Anna, reflected sufferings and devastation that stretched back to infancy, and which had one day to be released, however traumatically. Just as I had been the trigger that propelled Anna from an apparently hardworking student 'normality' into attempted suicide and madness eleven years before, so now I was the trigger – or at least the safety catch – for an uncontainable explosion inside her being.

I had to accept.

29

Thursday, 31 May 1973

'Wake at 9.15 after fitful night. Long talk with Anna in bedroom before I get up. She still convinced – as yesterday – that the Chinese are here, talks of Chinese Commander outside (police sergeant?), says they are waiting for her, that I am dying, that she has "betrayed" everybody, that our whole conversation is being broadcast, makes "sh" noises when I refer to the episode with the boys (embarrassment?).

'Obviously desperate to leave. Go for a walk, but little help. Does not like me touching her, though sometimes strokes me like an object.

'Cannot see how I can stand it for much longer, every hour of every day . . . Driving *me* insane!

'Curious how at one level she accepts she is schizophrenic – her word – and behaving madly, yet adamant that all her fears are "true". Stays upstairs before and after lunch – asks why I can't go and leave her?

'Almost tempted to, or vice versa; but in the end I am responsible for her. Who would believe me if she were harmed and I said to let her wander about in this state was right?

'Gunhilda comes at 4 p.m. Relieved – I feel I must get out – go to my study, collect German library books, take them to Kensington. Feeling oppressed, obstinate after what has happened. Janice Holmes also waiting for train, but we do not talk – though she knows all that is happening here from Joe's coming to play with Gabriel. At the next station she passes my compartment window – she blushes, apologizes for not having spoken to me: "I was reading a book. I hope you don't think . . ." Feel even more confused than she.

'At German Institute Library the woman asks after Anna. For the first time I am aware of my own presence, how I must look to others, so serious. Go on to see film by Borowycz: *Blanche*. Gruesome: yet such a wonderful film that afterwards I feel quite restored. In train I think over all the "possibilities".

Slowly am having to face the question whether Anna might not actually leave *me*: and in the present situation I feel more the "patient", than she: that it is my own "conventionality" that is under fire, my own growth that is at issue: Anna is striding forwards!

'Gunhilda meanwhile not made much contact with Anna – though no attempt on Anna's part to leave the house – makes me feel even more personally rejected.

'Gave Anna two Mogadon as we shall be alone in the house tonight. Sleeps, but up early.'

30

Friday, 1 June 1973

'Stay in bed most of morning. A friend comes at 2 p.m. and I go down to newspaper office till 4.30. Jill very sympathetic – says her mother was in mental hospital for six months after she was born. I felt grateful for her company – lovely blue eyes she has. Take Anna with me to library and local history archive. See Denis. A. very quiet but does not run away. Return home 6 p.m. Patty comes 6.20. Leave them with Miranda for theatre to see *Wild Duck*.

'About 12.45 when we get back. Anna asleep, but Patty awake. Stay up till 4 a.m. talking: tell her of fairground incident, my feelings of confusion, etc.: my conviction that it may, however, be the first step in Anna's own liberation. Yet sensing Patty's own convictions in that direction, pose the contrary view as well – whether one has the right to disturb so much – viz. tonight's Ibsen play. The danger of Anna gaining "herself" in the sense of self, but losing her children, losing me.'

What concerned me was the possible result of Anna's quest: that in making this journey of liberation she might shatter the one relationship which had informed her life for eleven years. It was a risk for both of us: and yet, ultimately, it was only a theoretical one. I was hurt and not a little angry at her 'rape'; but I still loved Anna – I didn't have any doubt about the depth of that.

Or did I? The danger surely was twofold; for if Anna's quest took her away from – beyond – me: who could say what other direction my own life would take, if I too put love and life to the test and negated them? It was uncanny how Ibsen's play related so closely to my own problem: namely, the amount of truth man can live with tolerably. Ekdal, the central character, is not fulfilled – but in a very real sense he is happy – and that happiness he imparts to those around him: his father, wife, child, lodgers . . . Who might say where Anna's and my own 'deeper selves' might lead us if we were liberated? And was it worth losing the happiness we had?

Patty couldn't answer that, and neither could I. I had to trust somehow that there *was* a pattern behind it all, which was not destructive and wouldn't bring tragedy as in Ibsen's play, but hope and growth. Living through Anna's psychosis had been an act of faith from the start. After everything it remained that.

31

Saturday, 2 June 1973

'Woke about 9. Anna clasping me, not wanting me to go away (I didn't know then that Patty had already suggested she go to the Community).'

We began to make love – the first time since Anna broke down four long weeks before. What it signified to Anna is impossible to tell; but for me it was symbol to many feelings: to the fact that Anna's psychosis had not diminished my physical and sexual attraction to her one scintilla; to the fact that the business of her 'rape', despite the shock, had not harmed my love for her. In looking after Anna at home I had wanted to prove to her that I accepted even her madness as part of her being, and loved her no less for it – and in making love to her that day I was at last able to show this proof in the most fundamental way that a man can.

For me, then, an equilibrium was restored. When Patty knocked, and suggested that after lunch and short walk in the park we should go to an Open House on the other side of London, I welcomed the idea. Anna, however, had ideas of her own.

The house was a large, Victorian white-stuccoed mansion. The At Home was in the basement. There were perhaps twenty people there when we arrived, all connected with Laing's work in some way.

'Anna very unwilling to enter spirit or conversation. Stands in corridor most of time.'

I found it difficult at first to make conversation, but after a while a group of us began to talk about theatre.

'Then Anna broke bottle. Dead silence everywhere. Clear up. Anna, in the bedroom, says quite touchingly: "Well, no one would talk to me!" But also: "Why don't you electro-shock me – but with anaesthetic?"'

It was impossible to know how seriously to take this remark. Patty's intention in inviting us there was to take Anna on to the Community afterwards if she would go, in order to see how she would react to a possible stay there. But when Patty now put the suggestion to her, Anna showed a marked disinclination, and I drove her home.

'On the way home ask if Anna wants to see the Buñuel film we had left prematurely the other day; nods in seeming assent; but how much she really understands of what I say is almost impossible to find out. In the end we go on, but in the City she whispers: "Could we go back?"

'I stop; but it is obvious it is not the film she wishes to go back to, it is the Open House, the broken bottle, a better "account" of herself . . .

'Peter rings and comes over. While waiting ask if Anna wants to go to bed. Nods. She seems cold, but is not interested in sex.

'Peter brings chicken and we have supper. Anna at first not wanting to eat her chicken, then saying: "This is Gabriel" about the leg as she gnaws it. Goodness knows what she means. She goes upstairs and Peter and I talk about his life – whether to share flat with his girlfriend, etc.

'Go to bed at 1 a.m.'

Peter and I had not really talked of Anna. Despite her statement she seemed relatively peaceful – anxious at least not to be left out, for she kept reappearing at intervals after the meal, from upstairs. Yet there seemed no sign of an end to the psychosis.

32

Sunday, 3 June 1973

'Roy Landis comes around 9. Anna opens the door for him (I was asleep and did not hear the knocking). From upstairs I later hear sound of tape-recorder in German – assume it is Anna who has put it on. ("Are you here?" she asks, surprised, as though she thought I had been taken away.)

'I go down about 11. It is the tape of Anna's mother that Roy has been playing – very emotional: period when Anna's brother was born, her difficulties living with mother-in-law. Very clear. At end R.L. suggests I or Anna tell him about the "incident" and he tape it. Anna quiet, wary of tape machine – I tell R.L. of her bugging fears, etc. R.L. leaves 1 p.m.

'Walk in park – bandstand, light music. Anna not liking me to hold her hand too much.

'Return 5 p.m. Go and play tennis, taking Anna with me.'

Afterwards, at home, I had a bath – and Anna joined me. We began to make love. I was both excited and awed by what was happening. I asked her what it felt like.

'Nice,' she said coolly.

'Interrupted by children arriving back at 8 p.m. Anna very excited. Thomas comes upstairs calling "Hello Daddy, hello." Seems terribly pleased to see us (as we are to see him). Gabriel too. Both kiss Anna when I ask them to – not afraid of her anymore – nor Anna of them! Thomas goes to sleep straightaway, Gabriel too excited. Very bronzed. Anna anxious that Satu not go out. "We must stay together," she repeats.'

33

Monday, 4 June 1973

'Thomas wakes at 5.45 a.m., pick him up, Gabriel wakes – then all go back to bed till 8.

'Gabriel goes off to school quite happily – Janice Holmes gives him a lift – and we come home. Think I ought to make a proper sandpit – would occupy me anyway! Start work, digging out larger area with Thomas. Anna sits at side, apparently quite happy, smokes, goes indoors occasionally only to reappear.

'After lunch go in the van to fetch more sand, etc. I notice Anna anxious to do things for Thomas she has not done before (since crisis began). He doesn't trust her or at any rate still clings to me – but how wonderful to see Anna wanting to communicate with him!

'Return as Gabriel comes up hill from school. How happy he seems to see us! All excited and curious about the mysterious "work" I am engaged on (which Satu has told him about). Together the three of us finish the sandpit wall while Anna sits and is "with" us.

'Tears from Thomas. Eventually I shout – Gabriel cries and Anna wants to comfort Thomas – such a "normal" situation!

'Supper and then bathe the children. Story. Thomas goes to sleep – Gabriel draws his picture of Harry from the story.

'"Dad, why don't you write a book of Harry stories?" he asks – then goes into how we could put our own covers on it, "sort of publish it ourselves," and he could take it to school.

'Anna does not actually take Mogadon (I learn later) that I give her – but sleeps perfectly.'

34

Tuesday, 5 June 1973

'We take children to school – Gabriel wants to take our Fischer model (of a lamppost-cleaning lorry-crane), but forgets it at last moment. Thomas pretends to be Harry ("terrible noise" he whispers and zooms off, followed by Gabriel).

'Return home, fetch cement and paving slab from builder's merchants for sandpit. Work slab in, Thomas helping, when Satu says Anna is gone.

'Take car, with Thomas, and look for her – try school, looking in playground, but no sign. Only when we return, some time later, Satu says school has phoned – Anna is there. Somehow I am not surprised.

'Go down in jeans to collect her – Thomas insists on coming with me. Headmistress obviously upset ("Can I call a doctor? She should really be in hospital. She's very unwell . . ."). Upstairs in staffroom Carol Burgess with her (alone)! Carol also very anxious that Anna see a doctor. I say we are facing this one out at home and will be seeing psychiatrist tomorrow. Carol argues for the mental hospital – "I didn't have ECT last time – it was a great relief to go there – I could take Anna on Friday – I go every Friday, I help there . . . Oh yes, she *must* go to hospital . . . Anna, would you like to go there?" (Anna shrugs.) "Oh, you see, she says yes – or she doesn't say no – she *must* go . . ."

'I take Anna home. Her eyes are a bit wild, will not talk. I know I have neglected her a little. "Why did you walk out?" I ask. "What did you want at the school?" "I wanted to fetch Gabriel," she says.

'At home I laugh to think how neurotic the *school* is about it: but nevertheless Anna's behaviour is no simple argument or even indication of wanting to stay at home; I cannot be complacent about it.

'We have lunch, then Satu takes Thomas to her friend near-by. I finish the sandpit. At 4 p.m. collect Gabriel from Holly, who gives us coffee and tells us about her new washing machine. Gabriel shows me the star he has got for reading – a sop for us? Draws warships with Duncan: Duncan infinitely careful, geometric and realistic, Gabriel's version sloppier but with a sense of life, of actual motion on the waves he has drawn. The hull stretches from end to end of the paper – as though the boat bursting to get out . . .

'At 5 p.m. a knock – Children's Welfare Officer! – on behalf of the headmistress! Explain the situation. Anna stares at her – still wearing my shirt (I said to her in the morning, go upstairs and change into a shirt, it's far too hot for a jersey; and she came down in one of my blue shirts – I had to laugh), but completely coordinated. Satisfy woman that I'm not mad, I think.

'Make supper, tell long story to children, put on radio. Anna goes out twice, have to call her back – turn off radio. She looks more haunted, less relaxed than lately. Still will not talk at all unless I force her – and then usual: "It's too late"; "Your family will have to pay for my . . ."'

'She must get so bored doing nothing all day I think – and begin reading David Cooper book again: but then come upon passage (underlined by Anna) about being with other people, but preserving separate identity. Feel calmer (as after reading Laing), and remember it is this sense of peace we are aiming at, not activity.

'Make hot chocolate and go to bed (without Mogadon).'

35

Anna was now in her fifth week of insanity. Laing's prognosis had run out: still there seemed little sign of emergence. On Wednesday, 6 June, we had arranged to go and see Landis, and fortune decreed we run into Laing himself – by complete chance.

'Sense Anna up very early – front door open. It is 7 o'c. Look out – white-haired lady leading Anna down the road from flats in her stockinged feet. Fortunate I happened to look out at that precise moment – they are on way to police station!'

We left home at 8 a.m. Anna was still very quiet, her eyes staring, and her hair greasy and unsightly. We took the train and tube; and coming out of the station saw R. D. Laing by shops over the road. Laing greeted us after a moment's hesitation. It was brilliantly sunny, about ten minutes past nine. Anna barely acknowledged Laing. He picked a hair off her suit-top, then she drew away, half-running, compulsively moving, like a troubled hen. Eventually we had to go and fetch her. I told him of the school episode and our problems – but he did not seem very talkative or even receptive to me, though concerned with Anna. I pointed out that his ten-day prediction had elapsed.

'What brings people "out of it"? I asked.

'"I feel I know that less than I did twenty years ago as a young doctor," he says a little sadly. "Some people seem to wake up one morning, or wake from a dream; some are very clear about what they have just been through, others not . . ."

'He keeps dropping his paper bags, of which he must be carrying five or six. I say there must be something psychological in that, and he is just about to answer ("Well, you know . . .") when he seems to stop himself.

'We part, go on to see Landis. Roy setting flowers, makes tea, smell of incense or whatever burning in his room from the Buddha figure on the mantelpiece. In corner sort of devotional prayer-mat – everything tidy – plum-ridged cord carpet, nothing on walls, windows open – fresher, different from all previous occasions. While Roy is out making tea Anna says to me: "I'm so obstinate!"

'How true!

'Have tea, but Anna saying nothing. I suggest I go for a walk, but Anna follows me, so we all go; take R.L.'s car – which won't start – to park. Sunshine quite brilliant and clear – in distance can see hills beyond London, in foreground the trees of the park. Like a ribbon, sandwiched in between, the high-rise flats and offices of London – quite thin in comparison with sprawling aspect – sensation of a strip of buildings in a valley, between escarpments.

'Talk to Roy while Anna wanders down hill – she is very "down in the mouth" still, her hands are rigid as during catatonic psychosis: pulls away a great deal. Tell him about school hysteria over Anna – says I should simply say Anna *is* under medical care.

'Anna moving out of visibility, so we walk down after her. Standing by public toilets. R.L. goes back for 11 a.m. appointment. We agree to meet him at 2 p.m. for visit to Community.'

The visit to the Community had been the purpose of bringing Anna to see Landis that day. Perhaps Roy wanted to see whether she responded to it at all, or whether members of the Community might take to her and provide more help at our own house. There was also the plan which Roy had mooted some days previously: that the whole Community should go on holiday to the country for a few weeks for a change; and that Anna, I, and the children should go too.

36

I stayed in the park till noon. Anna wandered about – a compulsive, desolate kind of ramble – looking back over her shoulder, frightened and lost. Yet to keep her by my side or even stay at hers was to restrain, restrict her, as of necessity I had to at home. It was an impossible situation. When she disappeared behind some shrubbery on one side of the park I had to call her back – and she returned like a child caught in the act – and yet mindlessly, robotlike, as though having to play this charade for want of anything better.

'Is it my failing patience or is there something automatic, robotic entering her behaviour?

'Walk slowly back. Buy fish and chips. At Landis's, have to cajole Anna to get her to eat them – cannot remember when she has been so "resistant". Is that a good sign?

'At 2.15 we drive to the Community. We were accompanied by an American observer, who ignored us; one house in demolition area stands frighteningly isolated among corrugated metal shields surrounding the acres of devastation. The one we go to, however, is in typical Edwardian road – house crumbling outside – old mattresses, etc., piled in front and bare floorboards. Kitchen at back decorated but piled high with rickety furniture, as is back yard. Sun still very hot and we sit outside on grass – on foam mattresses – that is to say members of Community, while Anna left completely alone, much as on Saturday at the Open House. Varying types, helpers and patients, almost all American.

'"I want to really get into the scene this time," I hear the observer saying to Roy. When he stares at me I say "Why are you staring at me?" and embarrassed he admits out of obstinacy because I "looked" at him. Fool. When at 4.30 I say we have to go he says: "You can get me through Roy's" – as though he were a social worker! And has not addressed a word to Anna.

'One of the helpers, nice – with curly dark hair – brisk. He has found us a farm flat near them in the country.'

It was a somewhat bewildering introduction to Laing's Community, the centre of enactment of Laing's highest ideals in the handling of schizophrenia. I tried to imagine Anna staying there, wondered in fact where she was. I asked the people in the house. No one knew. She had disappeared.

I felt ashamed again at having neglected her in a strange place, hated myself for having sat in the garden attempting to overcome my natural wariness, even hostility, to this strange, bleak, alien environment while Anna fled. Landis tore about the streets with me in his car, but there was no sign of her. Then I began to ask passers-by whether they had seen her.

'Asking people eventually pays off, find Anna in side road, R.L. takes us to station. Home at 6 p.m. – Anna still acting very robotlike – have to tell her twice to get out of train.'

37

That evening Anna still kept going to the door of the house, and it was difficult to get her to settle down for the night. She pretended to take her Mogadon tablets (I found them later), and slept very fitfully.

'I wake at 8 – she is still here, though tries to go over neighbour's wall at 8.30 – she sends her back. Take Gabriel to school, then mid-morning, while writing this diary upstairs – still extremely hot – she disappears. Hunt everywhere, but it is the neighbour who finds her in next street. Very quiet. Go for a walk with her in park. She looks at trees, the sky, will not sit down. Have lunch in garden; Anna sitting in kitchen but still making for the door every so often. Gabriel returns from school and helps sweep up in garden. 5.30 Patty comes. Talk little to her, then go and play tennis till 9.30. On way home visit a pub with disco for first time – so noisy my ears whistle for hours afterwards. Trying to lose myself? Or prove myself "normal"?

'Home at 11. Dan and Patty there. Talk a little. Dispute in kitchen about how much Anna is confused by way we ask questions – Dan attacking me a little! Anna out at least three or four times, despite walk with Patty. Worrying.'

Anna was clearly unhappy about having to stay in our house; but neither did she feel at home in the Community. Where would she feel safe? It was a question Anna herself would provide an answer to – and sooner than we could possibly have expected.

Friday, 8 June 1973

'Takes Mogadon and sleeps OK till 8 – still not taking off her clothes though. "Are you not dead?" is her first inquiry of the morning. "Oh God," I groan, realizing nothing is any better.

'Take Gabriel to school. Return 11 a.m. to find Patty has lost Anna half-hour before. Hunt everywhere, no sign. Patty goes home. Leave it over lunch and early afternoon, day still brilliantly hot – talked to Sarah about it, she still very anti "prison".

'At 3.45 note from Social Worker that Anna at local hospital.'

Had I been less proud I would surely have given in at this point, knowing that I had done my best. But the psychosis had lasted too long for me to act with discretion; I was both spiritually exhausted and yet somehow doubly defiant, obstinate. A game, a struggle, a war that hadn't been my own I now recognized – though perhaps phantasized – as very much my own. It would have signified only a temporary and at least honourable defeat to accept that Anna's particular brand of psychosis made it very difficult to cope with her without help; and that without such help it was extraordinary that we had come so far. There would no doubt be other times when, better prepared, we would be able to go right through psychosis at home, and emerge: but not this time.

But that wasn't how my mind worked. The biography, my very love for Anna, the shop ... Ingrained in me was some determined urge always to succeed at what was important to me, never to let up. This pride now began to turn from creative self-discipline, a deliberate extension of my sense of duty as a human being, into something rigid, unbending. I was like a general who sees that his army has reached the limits of exhaustion and yet wouldn't yield. At the local hospital I found a white-haired social worker who told me Anna had been admitted to the mental hospital until I could be found. She was at pains to point out that Anna had not been 'committed'.

Thus Anna came, after five weeks of madness in her own home, to the hospital which she had, in her previous lucid state, always insisted was wrong for her.

38

'Drive with children to the mental hospital. Anna not sedated but in pink dressing-gown and old blue nightdress – she holds it tightly round her body. Seems touched to see us when we arrive in ward, but within seconds closes off; and when I ask if she wants to come home she shakes her head. Later says she is a coward. Points to trees and says my family is up there! Will have to "pay for it", for what she has done. Wants to get dressed and leave, but not to come home with me. Finally disappears and goes and sits with other patients.

'"Mute", the charge nurse calls her. Asks for more information, we talk around the subject – tells me of changes being made in preparation for local authority management next year. Among other things mixed wards! Though initially dubious – gets Landis's name consistently wrong – about other doctor's care outside hospital, relatively sympathetic when I give him my own views.

Apparently Landis has phoned and stopped any drugs being given, other than sleeping tablets.

'Ask Anna time and time again; but seems to want to stay – even when children ask her to come home. At least she gives them a kiss though. Have to explain to them that Mummy feeling "safer", more "secure" there just at the moment, and no danger of her running out. Gabriel very sad at first – had wept when could not find me while I was talking to charge nurse.

'Drive home. Put children to bed. Watch crappy TV, make egg supper at midnight and write this. Tired. Curious to think, to feel sensation. First time Anna has been away from me for the night for five weeks of all this – excepting the fugitive night.'

39

Saturday, 9 June 1973

'Slept. Had felt how little reserves left last night, and when children climbed into my bed at 7.30 I awoke with feeling that I had been asleep, but had not cast off any of the burden. Ignore milkman's loud knock, far too early anyway. He goes away.

'Children clamber about – go in sandpit; very warm. Ring Landis at 8.45, no answer; he rings me at 9.30. Tell him about last night, Anna not wanting to come out. Explain how to get to the mental hospital. He suggests Patty, Dan, he and I "get together" to discuss the whole case some time next week.

'Children play outside. Anna's brother rings me at noon – suddenly says has seen similar case in his wife's sister and her husband; danger of the one simply dragging the other further down – main consideration should be getting Anna a proper task – viz., a decent translation.

'I don't feel angry at the time – surprised perhaps that B. should see the whole thing so simplistically. Wonder why? He says the more "understanding" one gives the more difficult for Anna to take it – which must be very true and has constantly been in my mind: yet somehow I don't think that is the point.

74

Anna is in just as mute a state without me (at the hospital) as with me – actually more so according to nurses. It is the weight of responsibility of facing up to herself that is the problem I feel.

'Children crying, terminate conversation – difficult to understand anyway why B. is saying this. To spare me?

'Make picnic lunch – children delighted and we eat it out of doors. Then go to play tennis. Gabriel and Thomas play relatively happily by the side while I am on court – good opponents. Tea at 5, then play with children, one more set with Bob, then shower and drive on with kids to hospital. Feel somehow lighter, less burdened. Children fall asleep on way.

'In ward Anna unchanged – hair beautifully brushed, still in old nightgown full of cigarette holes, but looking very attractive. Does not say anything, but not unpleased to see me. I ask if she wants to come home. At first she says yes, after asking if possible; but then declined in front of sister – who is also quite willing for her to go. I ask her if she knows why she does not wish to leave. "*Wegen des, was ich angerichtet habe* [because of what I have done]," she says when I beg her to speak. When I say children want her home, are in car, doesn't she wish at least to see them, she says: "I know they're all right with you."

'Wasn't I going to sit with one woman – or walk off with another? she inquires. I shake my head – sad to see her destroy herself this way after all we have been through these last weeks.

'"Got to have courage," I say.

'"*Das habe ich nie gehabt* [that's something I've never had]," she remarks ruefully.

'Children have already woken up when I go back to the car. Crying: must be careful never to give them feeling of abandonment now that Anna is not with me.

'Speak to Stephen on phone. Read paper, write this. Go to bed at 12.'

40

The next day was 10 June, a Sunday: 'Up at 8, children make jelly for Tim and Uncle Stephen and Auntie Bridget: "We're giving a sort of party," says Gabriel, and suggests we put fruit in the jelly.

'Sweep up garden, bonfire. They arrive late, eat at 2 – a meal Margo has cooked for us, herbal-spiced, aromatic and delicious. After lunch walk to park – flower garden, feed deer, then go on donkeys. Baby donkey. Converse with owner: says take 13 months to gestate!

'Children so sweet – though demanding on their bikes. Run down the hill. Overcast but not raining. Nice: yet *something* phony, if only that it isn't always like this, or that Anna is missing, or we are acting the role of sane people able to cope. But isn't that in fact the truth?

'Put children to bed and watch film on TV. Helen arrives at 10 – in state, crying, talking of suicide-longing, etc. Talk with her till 2 a.m. Poor thing.'

I hadn't visited Anna that day – the first time that we had been apart for a complete day since the beginning of her psychosis. I had planned to take Stephen at least. Perhaps we didn't go because I didn't want my brother to see her in hospital – wanted to keep up the 'role' of sanity and purpose, and was denying that Anna was actually there. Or perhaps I wanted Anna – knowing they wouldn't try to electro-convulse her or give any other such treatment on a Sunday – perhaps I wanted Anna to have a day free of me, and of the children, so that I could see its effect: whether she needed to get away from me, from us, from family obligations – or whether she wanted us there, missed me. I never recorded my actual motive as I saw it then. But either way the following, fateful days unfolded, unaffected.

41

Monday, 11 June 1973

'Took Gabriel to school – did not want to go really, the first time he had not wanted to since the start; but then I'd been making his Cutty Sark model for him since 7.30 when he woke, so he was naturally reluctant to leave it.

'Go on to the mental hospital at 11. Dr C., sitting in Sister's office. Nurse asks him whether he wishes to see me before or after I see Anna. Says after. Scarcely looks up. I say hello. Barely nods. First bad sign. Nurse says I look dazed – *exactly* how I feel.

'Anna looking equally well-kempt (hair brushed and shining), but longer in the face somehow– lips look a little chafed and sore. Still in old ward dressing-gown and nightdress despite the clothes I had brought her. Nurse shows us to private room – but occupied already. We go out a little, but Anna unwilling somehow, does not want to sit on bench, will not go more than 20 yards away. "Not supposed to" – undefined authority sitting in judgement on her (us). Again must press her to speak at all. When I ask if she wants to come home with me she makes a sort of smile-sniff as if to say: "If only, yes, that would be nice, but he doesn't *realize* why it's impossible." Tries to get in back of laundry van!

'Return to ward – find doctor has now left. Have him brought back. Ask him whether there is a misunderstanding, as I had been told on Saturday that he *wished* to see me on Monday. Evades point, says he must have been thinking of something else when he left.

'Starts interview – he asks for subsequent medical record since last breakdown – takes it down laboriously. I try to explain my point of view; but, as at the beginning, he reiterates Dr S. wishes to use "electrical treatment" and intravenous injections; so that I was left with an ultimatum: either Anna received ECT or she left the hospital. And that based on an "interview" they (he and Dr S.) had had with Anna that morning during which she refused to speak to them!

'I say, well, in that case I must take her away. He, surprised, says he has been told by S. that this was only course – must now consult again with Dr S. I go out.'

I was furious. Any hope of reaching an understanding with the hospital doctors whereby Anna might remain unmolested in the care of the hospital seemed to have been ruled out. I told the ward staff I would take Anna home with me, that I had been given an ultimatum.

'Nurses sympathetic, ask me to delay till doctor has consulted with S. Assure me nothing is going to happen directly. Nice staff nurse.

'Go for a walk with Anna to cool off – right round the grounds and back, then have snack lunch in canteen – Anna reluctant to go in there. When I ask if she knows why she doesn't wish to come home, says yes but cannot, is not permitted to tell me!

'Sometimes though she says she will come with me, "if that is what you want". Did not seem to want to go back to ward. I leave at 3 p.m. wanting to take her with me for safety's sake, but assured by charge nurse that they would inform me if any danger of E C T treatment being applied before tomorrow (Tuesday).

'To friends with children for tea. Beginning to feel weary.'

That evening I had a telephone conversation with Ted Grant, a friend and consultant psychiatrist – a conversation I shan't ever forget as long as I live. 'Says I have no legal leg to stand on if S. goes ahead with E C T – in due course, if I sued, I would have to prove damage. But he notes that in general he is against prolonging such schizophrenic or catatonic state because of damage it could cause ("not good to dwell in such a state too long"), and possibility of suicide. Does not advise me therefore to take Anna out of mental hospital. Danger of "catatonic stupor", where she would not eat, etc.'

Ted's advice was disturbing. He was a good friend. He knew Anna – had originally made it possible for her to have a year's psychotherapy at his hospital three years before; and this itself was the origin of Anna's determination to take responsibility for herself, not to be hospitalized . . .

I couldn't dismiss Ted's views. He had once seen Anna's case-notes. His concern about the possibility of suicide was salutary. 'I admire what you are trying to do, David,' he said, 'but I wouldn't take that risk with my own wife . . .'

But however much I respected Ted, my marriage to Anna was only half a marriage, our love only half-a-love unless we took this risk, unless we believed in a future not of caution and comfort. Anna and I needed change: the *possibility* of change.

'FEAR on Ted's part,' I wrote in my diary after the conversation. And as for taking Anna out of hospital: 'She has been "out" for five weeks already! Must make sure early tomorrow what is happening so that I can forestall them if need be by removing Anna. *I* must remain in charge, not doctors!'

42

The following day I typed out my refusal to give permission for electrical treatment, and my reasons for doing so. The letter was long-winded and over-emphatic, but it reflected my state of mind at that time, and it put, incontrovertibly, my views as husband of the 'patient':

To the Senior Consultant

Dear Sir,

This is to confirm in writing my response to your request that my wife, Anna Reed, be permitted to have electrical and intravenous treatment forthwith. I refuse to grant such permission on the grounds which I have stated to your junior assistant, namely:

(i) that such treatment would negate the positive contributions which psychotherapy at a psychiatric hospital and privately with Dr Roy Landis M D over the past three years has made in breaking the pattern of annual relapses suffered by my wife while previously treated by you at mental hospital and as an out-patient.

(ii) that my wife has always felt violated by such treatment on previous occasions, and that this sense of violation has been harmful to her subsequent improvement and stability. Before the current breakdown occurred she earnestly requested both Dr Landis and myself to shield her from such treatment again; both Dr Landis and I would be breaking an essential bond of trust if we were to renege on our word now, unless the situation were such that Anna's own life or the life of others were in danger.

(iii) that Anna's condition at present, her silence towards strangers and those whom she does not trust, may be seen as a natural sequence to a period of intense and agonizing 'breakdown' or 'breakout' at home in the past five weeks, and that as a human being she has a right to the relative peace and quiet nursing which your hospital has provided since her admission by error last Friday. I pay for such service in my weekly NH contribution, and I feel that after five weeks of caring for my wife without NHS assistance, and in considerably more intense states than the one in which my wife is currently living, I am not being unreasonable in asking your hospital to provide a temporary refuge for Anna without seeking unnaturally to precipitate her recovery.

(iv) that I plan to take my wife on holiday on 16 June 1973 where she will be under qualified psychiatric care and supervision, and that ECT and intravenous treatment at this stage would therefore be absurd in the short time available and without the possibility of continued or follow-up treatment.

(v) that my wife must be accorded the right to 'come out' of her silence in her own time without giving her or me the kind of ultimatums issued to me verbally by the doctor yesterday: namely that I must agree to electrical treatment or remove my wife elsewhere.

I must stress that I am deeply grateful for the kindness, the patience and understanding shown by the nursing staff in the ward since Friday to my wife, that my wife's contentment to stay there rather than to return with me both on that day and on each subsequent visit when I offered her the choice is a tribute to that care, and that my dissatisfaction is entirely with the adamant ultimatums issued on behalf of Dr S. to me yesterday. I hope that this letter clarifies my position in this matter, and that it reveals the desire not to interfere in professional procedures but to preserve the kind of integrity and human patience which in the long run will be the keys to permanent recovery on the part of my wife and a marriage that will stand the strain of schizophrenia.

Yours faithfully,
David Reed

The letter was given to the Assistant Matron, who put it in Anna's file. It was a plea for support – and a death warrant.

43

Wednesday, 13 June 1973

'Took children in evening to the hospital with tennis rackets. Anna clearly not better, but somehow I feel such despair that I say I will take her home – have her dressed. Assistant Matron intervenes, rings S., begs me not to. Go through ECT palaver again – though not the primary problem for me. Suddenly, after not having spoken at all to the woman, Anna sits down at the desk and asks very quickly and urgently: "What would *you* like me to do?"

'So she stays the night, while Matron gives full assurance that no ECT, etc., will be given. Tremendous relief really – and for the first time since last Friday I realize what a burden one lets oneself in for in taking on an insane person – and how extraordinary we should ever have got this far.'

There is nothing in my diary to explain my reference to ECT treatment not being the 'primary' problem for me. What was?

44

I suppose in truth I had been shaken by Ted's warning. The weeks of looking after Anna at home had definitely taken their toll. I wanted help: I wanted someone who would understand, who would see Anna's condition not as an isolated phenomenon but as a challenge, especially to my marriage. I didn't want to fight authority, I wanted help. Perhaps in intending to take Anna with me to the country at the end of that week I wasn't only protecting her from what I considered unnecessary and harmful electro-convulsive therapy, I was registering my own hurt, the same wound that I had felt at the start of Anna's breakdown when Landis refused to concern himself with me, the failure of the hospital to acknowledge me as in any way concerned with Anna. Somehow I felt that it was I who had kept Anna alive all the years since her first suicide attempt; and I wanted support, a basic recognition. The nurses were gentle and sympathetic listeners when I spoke, but they didn't represent power or authority in the ward or hospital. Archaically only the doctors did that, and they wouldn't even see me! No doctor at the hospital ever replied to my letter, no doctor there ever spoke to me again.

The days went by. I managed to stave off ECT therapy. Anna began slowly to talk more. On Friday I collected her from the ward at 1.45 in the afternoon. She was dressed and very quiet. I had to sign a form saying that I was taking Anna out of hospital 'against medical advice'. I think I was frightened: for a full week I had not had to look after her, the true strain had become clear to me in that interval. Once again I was taking entire responsibility on myself, with very little support.

At the same time a strange courage rose in me. We were going to the country. Landis would be there. Patty and Gunhilda, too. We would not be alone. There would be the change of scenery, a part of England that we had never seen before. Only courage would – could – see us through.

At home I picked up the children and loaded the last bits and pieces, including Gypsy, our cat. She had no desire to stay in the little cat-basket. She broke the string tying it, and sat behind my shoulder, eyeing both the road and the side window; but after a while she settled down.

45

The journey lasted five hours. 'Found farm only after numerous mistakes. "Are you sleeping in there?" Anna asks, motioning to Satu's room. Nevertheless, she seems to sleep all right.

Saturday, 16 June 1973

'Woken this morning circa 8 a.m. Anna gets up, children get into my bed. Get things from van, take a bath – children get in. Anna seems reasonably well – still refuses anything one offers though. Drove to village – she stays in car while we shop. Thomas makes frantic noise over who should carry the eggs – he thinks of course that he should! Must be difficult for Anna to listen to him in such a state.

'Drive on to the cliffs. Park and climb hill with children. Anna stays in car, wanders about the car park – but comes up a little to help Thomas down last slope when we return.

'We walk on a little – high cliff. Very hot. Looking out across the sea, hazy in distance, and the green rolling hills about us almost eerie. I went down steep slope myself to see if negotiable path to the bay below – found Anna following me and reluctant to return when I decided it was unsuitable for the children. Very stiff again – as though braced for suicide. Had to encourage her to go back in front of me.

'Same too when we found the proper path down to the cove – suddenly she began sliding down almost sheer hillside. She had fallen behind a little, so I wasn't sure if she might not simply have panicked – but she'd left her shoes back on the path and didn't like me fetching them or "catching" her as she slid to the path through the bracken. The beach unexpectedly sandy – at least, a shingly sort of grey sand, like gravel.

'Very hot, slight breeze. We went down to the water and lurid sea, jumping from boulder to boulder. Anna convinced we would not be able to "get out" – or if so, only when "tied up" and "dragged away". By whom? People who would "come by boat". But who would they be? People "got" by Satu . . . !

'Poor Anna – her face now thin, her hair matted against her skull. Her eye-sockets deep, etched out . . . FEAR.

'We stay till 5 p.m. Another tantrum from Thomas, who had been asleep for a little on Anna's lap.

'Came home. Anna eating hardly any supper – because Satu had cooked it perhaps? Or too agitated. She puts out the farm cat who comes up from downstairs – to do the "right" thing – or because she identifies with it?

'Puts on nightdress when children go to bed. Hope she will sleep.'

But she didn't.

46

Sunday, 17 June 1973

'Though she went to bed at the same time as the children, Anna didn't seem to sleep – heard her padding around till midnight when I turned in. She was lying on the floor beside the bed. We got in. I held her hand, and I fell asleep.

'The next thing I knew I was awake with a start. It was fairly light. Anna was standing over the children's bed with a pair of red tights drawn about Thomas's neck. He must surely have had time to cry out, for otherwise I cannot imagine how I could have woken up at that precise moment. Seeing me sit up Anna did not stop, but simply pulled tighter her strangle-hold, with an expression of haunted helplessness, unable to stop. I roared "Anna!" so loudly my throat hurt for hours afterwards. She let go.

'Gabriel woke, and both children cried. I leaped out of bed and removed the tights from Thomas's neck. When I asked Anna why she was trying to kill him she said: "To stop him being tortured."

'I remember how yesterday on the beach Anna seemed to keel over in despair, her face contorted as though trying to cry. But this . . . this.

'It was only after an hour that we went back to sleep, after I had asked Anna to promise not to do it again. "They look so beautiful," she answered, looking at them. Gabriel had put his arm round Thomas's waist, and Thomas his own round Gabriel's shoulders. "*Fünfzehn Minuten Frieden: dann unten mit den Hunden* [fifteen minutes' peace: then down below with the dogs]," she said without elaborating.

'Later, when we woke and the children played, Anna asked me to take Gabriel away – as though she wished to keep Thomas with her for some undefined purpose which could not be fulfilled as long as I was present.

'A *terrible, terrible* situation. Thinking of how I can now ask the mental hospital to take her back. And ECT? How long can we go on like this? Alternatively she ought to stay in the Community. Or is this me retreating?'

Who could believe it? I was confused myself. A group from the Community dropped by to introduce themselves in the morning. I felt their foreignness to my/our situation, that they could have no notion how frightening it was, the true terror of a child's life being threatened ... They seemed all so very much concerned with their own equilibria, their own psyches, like a group of hippies trying to 'tune into' the countryside. It wasn't that I took exception to them as individuals: only their fatuousness as 'helpers' in a dilemma as terrifying as this. I told some of them what had happened in the night. They showed not the least concern.

Nor had Landis arrived from London.

Ought I to have abandoned the 'holiday' then and there? There could be no mistaking the seriousness of Anna's condition. What had once been only a threat to the children (the night she reported to the police station that she had murdered them) had now been physically enacted – at least attempted. If I hadn't woken?

It was not simply obstinacy that made me continue though. Perhaps it was the contrary, a *new* determination. On the one hand I saw remote ECT-favouring doctors, on the other the idealistic self-concern of Landis's Community. Between them there was Anna; and more then than at any other moment in her psychosis I felt her need. There could be no doubt that in attempting to kill Thomas she was reaching the brink of extinction – for Thomas she loved without anxiety, reserve, or guilt. Thomas represented her loving, open self: 'moon-face' as she called him. To kill him meant surely to kill the thing most good within herself – I felt despair could go no further, no deeper, or be more cathartic than that. And I felt no one else could or was even willing to understand or to help. Landis had not even arrived ...

'Sky at first misty and very wet outside. Clears about 11 a.m. Went down with Anna and the children to stream at bottom of field. Played there, as once I had in a brook as a child myself. Gabriel trying to dam the stream, Thomas sitting on my lap, throwing in twigs, swinging on gate. Idyllic somehow.

'But Anna still very frightened, afraid. Stiff and poised again as once before in London – wants to cross the river – keeps simply stepping into stream up to her knees, disregarding shoes, trousers. Then tries to "disappear" as she calls it, downstream – crouching in bank, picking way across stones, wading through water – like a very frightened deer.

'We go up to farm at 1.30. Patty passes with a friend. Tell her about last night. At first cannot believe Anna was serious.'

I was alone and yet I felt I still could not give up hope. Perhaps, too, what had happened represented an end-point. I don't think I was conscious of this intellectually, but underneath I must have felt such a possibility, otherwise I could not have gone on. After lunch I decided to go down to the sea.

'Gravelly beach by small harbour. Tide out. Sit by rockpool, exposed. Anna talks a little after a while. Doesn't want to as she says everyone can hear. Also pointless because I should have killed her. Why? Should take Gabriel with me to save myself. Why? In order to marry Elizabeth! Crying as she says this.

'Explain it's not true, encourage her to look within herself for origins of her fear. Extraordinary how half-normal in conversation with me she can be. Talk about attention-seeking aspect of conspiracy fears. But what can I do? How can I control them? Anna asks. By talking about them, not bottling them up, by trying to accept them as phantasies and to look for their origins, I say. But when I have them I believe them, Anna explains.'

For the first time in six long weeks we began to talk normally to one another.

'Search for crabs, show Thomas round harbour. Sky almost cloudless now, though wind whipping up oncoming tide.

'Drive back to farm. Leave children with Satu, go over to the Community's farmhouse, across ford, and up winding lane. Fantastic views over green valley and the moors at the head. Only couple of people there, not talkative. Could be a film if you romanticized the situation, or quiet reality if you accepted it as such. Sat outside for ½-hour. Utterly peaceful – farmer herding cows in with help of three dogs on far slope of valley (for milking?).

'Come back to farm. Anna very quiet. Children not asleep, though in bed. Turned on TV to see Humphrey Bogart and

Laurel Bacall in *To Have and Have Not*. Children came and watched it beside me. Anna watching a little from door, strangely riveted.

'Put the children to bed when it's over.

'Then Anna, in kitchen, suddenly starts emerging.'

I could scarcely believe it, it had been so long in coming.

47

However, one day she arrived, punctually and amazingly transformed. For the first time in my experience of her she was dressed with at least ordinary care and without that disturbingly odd appearance in dress and manner that is so characteristic of this type of person but so difficult to define. Her movements and her expression had, unmistakably, *life* in them. She began the session by saying that she realized that she had been cutting herself off from any real relationship with other people, that she was scared by the way she had been living, but, apart from that, she knew in herself that this wasn't the right way to live. Obviously something very decisive had happened. According to her, and I see no reason to doubt this, it had arisen out of going to see a film. She had gone every day for a week to see the film *La Strada*.

This passage from Laing's *Divided Self* came back to me quite suddenly. I had asked him in Hampstead what brought people out of psychosis, and he had said it was impossible to answer. Yet just as Marie in *The Divided Self* seemed freed by the experience of a film, so too it happened with Anna. When I asked her what had brought her back to reality she said it was the newspaper – a copy of the *Guardian* lying in the television room – and the Bogart film which 'reminded' her.

Laing's patient had been moved by the heroine of *La Strada*, who, despite the awfulness of her life, does not 'cut herself off from life'. Whether Anna identified with a phantasy of herself in *To Have and Have Not*, a woman who has been through all the degradations and humiliations of life but can still act with faith and courage, I do not know; but like Laing, I have no reason to doubt it. From that moment Anna was a different person. 'Why didn't you tell me . . .?' she asked, as though she was coming out of a long sleep, a dream. She was just beginning to 'remember' things, like a patient emerging from amnesia. To test her I asked if she remembered what had happened the night before.

'"Oh yes," she says. She had wandered outside (so it was true what she had said about this earlier!), gone into barn, wanted to throw herself down from the upper floor ... then had come inside and started to strangle Thomas. On the beach when I asked about this, she said she wasn't sure if she would really have done it, depended on resistance ... and that the colour of the tights was significant, symbolic ...

'"If I hadn't done that to Thomas I would have thrown myself down," she says. I remember her first explanation: "To stop him being tortured."

'She seems utterly lucid. Patty comes with James, young blond boy with gold-rimmed glasses, rather golden-looking. Anna tells Patty too that she is emerging. After Patty and James go, says Mary Barnes a saint – doesn't eat, fasting, that's why she was so thin and shaky.

'Make light supper with tin of salmon. Anna says cannot remember what has happened since she came back from Germany with Gabriel – over 3 months ago! Still a little muddled. Mentions that Ted had once told her her illness going in a spiral.'

Eventually we went to bed about midnight. It looked as if, after all, the journey down to the country had been worth it. Anna had come through, had gone through her own madness – and had survived!

48

19 June 1973

Dear Matron,

I wanted to write and tell you how things have gone since Friday when I took Anna away from the hospital 'against medical opinion' ... We drove straight down here.

That night was perhaps the worst in the entire traumatic six weeks we have been through. I woke up at about 5 a.m. to see Anna standing over Thomas's bed with a pair of children's tights around his neck and attempting to strangle him. He must have cried out because otherwise I cannot imagine how I could have woken up at that precise moment. Though I was now staring at her she seemed unable to stop and I had to shout at the top of my lungs and leap out of bed.

You can imagine my feelings once I had persuaded Anna to lie down again. Every instinct told me it was madness to try and see out this trip alone; yet every new disaster has paradoxically confirmed my belief that only by truly confronting such insanity – including the possibility of suicide and even infanticide – can we drive beyond the recurrent schizophrenic pattern of temporary well-being and break-down. I took several deep breaths, and after about an hour went back to sleep.

It was raining on Sunday morning – as though the weather were somehow aware of our tribulations. With the children we went and played in the river below the farmhouse – but Anna seemed no quieter in herself – murmured she had been out in the night in the barn, and began compulsively to disappear down the stream, cowering in the bends and wading knee-deep in her shoes where there were no stones to step on. In the afternoon the wind blew the clouds from the sky and the sun shone fearlessly above us. In the evening when the children were in bed, turned on the TV – yes, we have TV here! – to see Humphrey Bogart in *To Have and Have Not*. Anna watched from the door. I felt a little as though I were neglecting her by doing so, but I felt so exhausted I just wanted to get away – even into the mesmeric phantasy world of Hollywood.

How extraordinary, then, that when I switched the set off Anna should quietly announce she was 'emerging'!

It was as though something in the film had triggered the spark we have all been waiting for. Did she see herself in the role of Lauren Bacall? Or did the phantasy world of the film give her a sudden perspective on her own planetary-realm?

I don't suppose we shall ever know. R. D. Laing quotes a similar example in *The Divided Self* – where a compulsively hostile and indifferent patient suddenly becomes 'normal' after seeing Fellini's *La Strada* – about a girl who starts living with a circus showman.

I went to bed wondering whether it was 'real'; and apparently Anna still had wide-awake visions of descending into hell. I had arranged for the children to sleep in another room with the door locked, but it didn't prove to have been necessary; Anna awoke the most 'normal' woman I have ever known her to be. I heard her singing in the bathroom, the children warmed to her as if nothing had ever happened to disturb the relationship between them; and together we went down to the river where only the day before Anna had cowered and run away – apparently in the notion that by crossing it we had disturbed a whole network of locally inter-related I R A farms as she told me later! She bubbled now as fast and contentedly as the water itself: there was no holding her back. My heart was alive too with pleasure – of relief and joy, and no little pride. We had come through!

Will it last? Is this now the beginning of recovery? Of a path towards a new and better sanity?

Last night Anna went quiet again in bed, as though once again she were 'sinking': perhaps the night is still frightening for her. This morning she is up and making breakfast for us all – indeed I have to be careful she doesn't take on too much too early. But somehow I think we *are* through. Not a road I think many could or should take with all its dangers; yet if life is given for more than just 'coping'; if growth means not repetition or comfort but adventure and courage, means going beyond our known selves . . . well then perhaps we are getting somewhere and are not easily to be mocked by clinical experts whose own personal development may be prematurely stunted.

Anna has said so many nice things, so many appreciative things about the way she was looked after in the ward that I would like to add them – or the sense of them – to this letter. Perhaps you would care to show it to the nursing staff there – even add it (or a photocopy) to the 'notes'. It is always possible that Anna will be 'back' – I am under no illusions and wish to make no predictions. We shall see.

Sincerely – and gratefully,
David Reed

49

I sent the letter. I was so joyful and proud – so grateful to everyone who had helped, who had tried to help, who had sympathized and listened. To see Anna that first morning after her emergence in the stream with the children – oh, she was ecstatic, excited! It felt as though she had been away for six months, she said; though if I pressed her she could remember most incidents, how they had appeared to her at the time.

And the boys she slept with at the fair? Oh, it was nothing, it was trivial, it was part of her phantasies at that time – I should not even think about it. What was important was that we were together, we'd come through together . . . How glorious the countryside, how wonderful the farm. How ever had I found it, she wanted to know. How much did it cost? But eighteen pounds a week was nothing, it was a godsend! And Satu? – was Satu all right? She felt it was Satu who had looked after 'us' throughout – had I paid her the right money each week – no, five pounds was too little, we must pay her the extra, because she'd been working twice the normal hours . . .

Anna couldn't have been more lucid, more rational, more aware, more *sane*. In the afternoon we drove to the village and she stayed with Patty in her cottage while I did shopping, etc., with the children: and how happy she was when I returned!

We bathed the children, put them to bed. We had supper and went to our own bedroom. We made love. I'd never experienced it with this passion since the time we first knew each other – quite wildly. We took off into space. There were just the bones, the thinness and the freshness and the smoothness of our bodies. We had no contraceptives. Anna turned over, and I came.

Then there was silence. Anna wouldn't speak. Her ecstasy seemed suddenly to have frozen into a strange kind of trance. She went to the bathroom, came back, but there was something wooden, an almost somnambulistic rigidity in her eyes as she stared ahead or through me.

I wondered whether I'd gone too far, assumed Anna could throw off a psychosis which had lasted six weeks in as many hours. I recognized that it would probably be much more difficult, more complicated than that – that we must take things gently. . .

However, Anna awoke the following morning, 19 June, as joyful and happy as the morning before. She made breakfast for us all – for the first time in six weeks! – and we went for a long walk across the river, up the valley, then back across the ford there and home through the meadows to the farm. Patty was waiting there. She asked if she could stay with us now, in the living-room, as had originally been planned. And Anna – Anna so happy, so wonderfully happy and proud – said no, she didn't wish to be inhospitable, but she'd only just come out of the long nightmare, it was all so new, so fresh, and she just wanted to be alone with me for a few days, perhaps then . . .

Of all the decisions made over those six weeks it was, paradoxically, this one, made in clear, in ecstatically clear mind, that was to prove the most fateful.

We went indoors; Satu had made lunch; then Anna insisted I go into the bedroom with her . . . She was excited – she wanted me to make love, without time even to take off our clothes. The children came and tried the door, I had to send them away. Again, as we came near to orgasm, Anna turned over.

And again, after we had finished, Anna went into a kind of trance. Satu had made coffee. Mary Barnes had come to see us and was waiting in the living-room. There was a crash: Anna had smashed her cup on the floor in the children's room. When I went in she stared daggers at me and left – went down the stairs and outside.

50

Should I have followed her? I was perplexed and went in to Mary Barnes. I said, 'Mary, you have been through this yourself. Anna "emerged" late on Sunday night. She's been ecstatically happy since then; but she's suddenly angry now, has run out. What's behind it? Does it mean she hasn't really come through yet, at least not completely?'

And Mary Barnes – thin, very frail, drinking only warm milk with honey – looked at me with eyes of such compassion.

'If it happened so suddenly, then that's not a good sign . . .' she began.

Mary left a little later. I felt confused, upset, guilty that I'd done something wrong, had taken advantage of Anna – and yet it was she who had wanted so urgently to make love. Should I have said no?

I felt tortured – and upset, disappointed, perhaps even a little

92

fearsome, wondering if I could possibly last out another period of psychosis if it should go to that.

We stayed a while in the flat. Satu went for a walk, and I decided eventually to take the children to the sea. Then Gabriel wouldn't come, I grew angry; we were going up the path by the farmhouse to the van, with Gabriel crying, when Anna reappeared!

She was utterly composed. She soothed Gabriel, went and fetched the boat he wanted to take with him; but said she wouldn't come with us. She wanted to lie down and have a rest. She was as normal as I had ever known her in my life, no longer even excited, but quite calm. She didn't say why she had broken the cup or gone out; but whatever it was, it was over. She kissed me and went indoors.

I took the children to the seafront, we played 'tempting the tide' by the harbour, climbed into fishing boats lying dry on the mud. On the road down, not far from the farmhouse, we met Roy Landis coming up – he had just arrived from London. I told him very briefly about Anna and asked if he would call in to see her. He said he wasn't sure if he would have time as he was going on to the Community farmhouse. (Patty and Mary Barnes were with him in the car.) But, he added, his wife was coming down the following day. It would be her birthday, and they were going to celebrate it with a party. He wanted Anna and me to come to it if we would.

It was latish when I drove home. Roy had been there for two hours with Patty and Mary Barnes; yet Anna seemed quiet and depressed.

I made supper for the children, put them to bed. Anna would eat nothing and was completely silent. Finally I made her sit with me at the table in the kitchen and begged her to tell me what was wrong.

She looked at me distantly.

'Will you let me see the children afterwards?'

'After what? What are you talking about?'

'After the divorce.'

I was flabbergasted. How could I possibly summon again all the patience, the understanding, the reassurance she needed?

'Anna,' I started, 'I'm just too tired, too exhausted by these months of trial to have the strength now to argue with you, to show that you're wrong, that you're inventing this . . . You've just got to believe me when I say I wouldn't, I simply *couldn't* have gone through the last six weeks unless I did love you, unless I wanted us to live together, to go on living together . . .'

I persuaded her to lie down, and I lay with her, holding her hand, stroking it, trying to help her to relax. But she wouldn't sleep; and as the hours went by it became more and more difficult for me to keep awake.

51

Finally I dozed off, and awoke to see Anna limping around the bed. I asked her what had happened. She said she had fallen out of the window. But when I got up there was no sign that she'd opened the windows in our bedroom or anywhere else in the flat. I got her to come back to bed again, and lie with me, comforting her.

Some time later we heard the noise of a car. Anna sprang out of bed and over to the window, and started talking of needing to go with the car. It had come for her, she had missed it . . . I said, 'Look, it's just the farmer going off to milk the cows.' I looked at my watch. It was somewhere between 6.30 and 7 a.m. I'd had barely half-an-hour's sleep. I felt weary beyond all measure. I coaxed Anna back into the bed, covered her, though she would not undress. Then I fell asleep.

There was a sound of someone talking, and I turned over, finding it difficult to open my eyes. It sounded like Anna in the bathroom, there was water running.

'Run a bath for Mummy, run a bath for Mummy,' I could hear her saying to herself, as though to a child. It seemed dark still, the curtains were drawn.

I called: 'Anna, come back to bed. Darling, what are you doing?'

And then she was standing in the doorway; standing there like a child who has done something silly.

Part Two
Origins

1

When I first met Anna I was barely eighteen. I was due to start at Cambridge the following October; in the meantime it was early summer. I was spending a semester at Munich University and living with a friend from school.

We rented a small chalet on the outskirts of town. For £70 I had bought an ancient Volkswagen, and thus at the week-ends we could drive all over Bavaria and the Austrian mountains.

My German teacher had recommended the town, which was one of the few to have preserved its pre-war character despite the ravages of bombardment. It clustered about its main avenues and gardens, the river and old city gates, its town hall and cathedrals. It had blue trams, elongated and thin, and on a clear day you could see the Alps in the distance. Theatre, opera, cinema were among the best in Germany – as well as museums.

I was unhappy at home and relished this freedom after the restrictions of school. I did very little work apart from going to lectures and seminars; and it was in one of the latter that I met Anna. She came in late, sheepish, shy and incredibly beautiful.

Anna was then twenty-four. Born in 1937, she was almost two when her father was called up, barely four when he was killed on the Russian front. Her brother came into the world only months before her father died; she remembered going into her mother's bedroom and finding her weeping over the telegram. Because her mother necessarily neglected her for the baby, she came to feel that she had killed her father: his death was an expression of her guilt-feelings, her hostility towards her mother and her infant brother.

Anna's childhood was marked by extreme loneliness. First there was the nightmare of bombing in Hanover, and then the flight from her grandparents' home in Posnania before the Russians. The family ended as refugees, in a tiny village near Lüneburg, and for years were treated as such.

There they lived alone with her mother's sister above the village school. Anna's mother had to work from morning till night in a shop eight kilometres away, and Anna soon had to supplement their meagre income by working in the fields for local farmers – collecting dung, gathering potatoes and turnips, picking blackberries. She worked hard at school but made no friends.

Finally, after six months in a children's home, her mother took her to Hanover with her in 1949. There Anna entered Volkschule; and in 1950 grammar school. She learned English for the first time and worked at week-ends as an assistant waitress at an ice-cream café. She was pretty, with a small delicate head, fine thin hair, and intelligent dark eyes. Physically she had already grown into a mature woman, with soft skin, large breasts, and a slender figure. She was chronically shy. She made no friends at grammar school either, though she did have an affair with a boy. When Anna's great-aunt heard of it, she predicted that Anna would 'end on the streets'.

The following year Anna took her Abitur, passed with honours, and after spending the summer at an international youth camp in Sweden, she matriculated at the University of Munich, some 400 miles from home.

Eight semesters passed before I met her. She became engaged to a Baron, a student at the Munich Academy of Art; but when I first talked to her I knew nothing of this or her past. I was attending a seminar on the history and meaning of jazz, and Anna came in, towards the end of the session, wanting to speak to the lecturer. He asked her to sit with us until the end. She had her hair combed back and tied with a green ribbon, wore a green pullover, a checked skirt, and simple black shoes. Her forehead was strong, prominent in that small delicate face, somehow bursting with intelligence. Or was it her eyes – deep set, a deep, dark brown that pierced you, and an aura of shyness, of gentleness, of suffering and of love? I could not take my eyes away.

There is a beauty which transcends conventional aestheticism.

There is the beauty of the spirit made manifest in the bone and in the flesh. Oh Anna you were so spoken for by your physical being! It spoke a magic, magic of tenderness and of sensitivity, of frailty and yet intellectual penetration, that bound me to you from that first moment in Munich in the little lecture room above the marble concourse. Oh, I knew frailty was precarious. I wanted to give you strength, to give you courage. I wanted to because your own being so filled me with joy! To know you was to be grateful for being alive. Oh Anna I loved you as I could never love another – never so completely, so utterly. I could never cherish anyone as I came to cherish you, at the age of eighteen, in the late spring of 1962.

2

Anna disappeared at the end of that seminar. But she must have noticed my distracted attention, for she returned the following week, and this time for the full three-hour session. In the interval she went out onto the balcony overlooking the concourse, and we began to talk.

She told me she was in her ninth semester, studying German philology and literature for a doctorate. She wore jeans this time, and a black anorak with red lining. Only her lips were made-up, and her eyebrows pencilled. Otherwise her small delicate head seemed to shine. Her skin was like a child's, quite perfect; her hair thin and combed back a little to give it more fullness.

I hardly dared hope that she might be interested in a mere boy, so much younger than herself. We resumed our places. At the end she again disappeared. I went down the main marble steps and found my flat-mate outside, waiting for me to drive him home. A friend from the seminar was with me and we talked for a moment. Then I saw Anna by the far wing of the university, wheeling her bike out of the basement shelter.

She began to cycle past. It was now or not at all. She might never reappear in the seminar. I couldn't stir. Yet this fear that I might never have another chance made my feet move. My head was in my heart and my heart was in my shoes. I had no idea what I could say. I stopped her, stood before her. I can remember today the way she supported the bicycle, with her hands on the handlebars and her feet on the ground, quizzical and cool. She seemed so small behind the large-framed, broad-tyred, basketed bicycle.

'What is it?' her dark eyes demanded.

'I . . . I was wondering if we could meet sometime,' I stuttered. She searched my face again, seriously.

'What have we to talk about that can't be said here?'

Somehow I weathered her gaze, insisted. She scribbled her name and address on the back of a used envelope – a fine, darting handwriting – and we arranged to meet the following morning.

3

It was a Saturday. There was little traffic. I found the cinema on the corner of the Prinzregentenstrasse, and the petrol station further down that road, towards Moabit where the No. 9 tram ran. I turned left. The house was huge; it took ages for Anna to come down.

We went up to her room. This was in the attic, which had been illegally converted. She didn't pay much in rent, but the room was tiny, with only a single narrow skylight open to the sky. The roof sloped dramatically. There was room only for a bed across the end, a bookcase, worktable, upholstered stool, and washbasin beside the door.

The bed was covered with a blue blanket, and served as settee. I sat there, Anna made coffee in hand-painted black-and-white vertically striped cups, and what we talked about I can't remember – only that she listened to my excitement and seemed to know that I was in love.

Time stood still. At half-past one Anna became anxious, and told me she was going to be collected. By her fiancé.

The word, the idea, hardly touched me: rather I felt excited, it made the situation more dramatic. I was standing in front of her, preparing to go, not knowing how to say good-bye. Then she simply reached up and buried herself in my arms.

I held her as though I had waited all my eighteen years for this moment – for I had. I had known nothing like it.

'You must go,' Anna whispered. She took my face between her hands and kissed me.

If ever in the years that followed I questioned Anna's love for me, or wondered whether I had taken her away from a country and a man who were hers, I had only to remember her then – that kiss and that whisper.

All my life at school – preparatory and public – I had formed intimate relationships with a single friend, with whom, as with my twin, I would become inseparable. I don't think schoolwork ever really interested me: what I lived for was the exploration of human affection and companionship – sharing, talking, being, doing things together, arguing and quarrelling: proving, every moment, the bounds and potentialities of love. I think I always had one major love-relationship going while I was at school, right until the end. By that time, though, sexuality had begun to enter. The shadows of good and evil, of desire and longing, stretched into my growing. I became aware of a sexual self that had not previously existed: the wild, brazen stirrings within.

In my last year I went on a summer course to Germany – and fell for a fellow-student. She was French, older than me, already engaged to be married. We decided to live together for the duration of the course. At nights we slept together, but we did not make love – I doubt if I should have known how. But she was the first mature woman I came to know intimately, and for me it was a decisive step. Not only was it a way of freeing myself from the homosexual and homoerotic limitations of school, it was also a way of escaping my father's high expectations, my parents' very English vision. It was a way of establishing an independence not only emotionally, but also culturally. I began to read French literature as though it were my own. From there to Munich, the following year, to the dark-eyed princess of my dreams was but a very short step. I never hesitated for a moment.

There was a note on my car the following Monday. We began to meet in the university refectory, and have coffee together down the narrow road, at the shop overlooking the English Garden. We attended lectures together. I was head over heels in love and, though six years older, so was Anna. I cherished every second with her, she touched my heart in such a way that I was utterly defenceless, every feeling of goodness and warmth I kept safe for her. She awoke in me a sense of complete masculinity, joyful and ecstatic, that I had never known in my existence before. Perhaps my love gave her a strength too. She excelled in her seminars, passed her driving test against all (and well-founded) scepticism; and then she asked, as I planned to drive through France and Spain in the summer vacation, if we could go together.

It was to be the most extraordinary and wonderful journey of my life – topographically, emotionally, spiritually, and sexually. During those six weeks in the summer of 1962, at the age of eighteen, I reached manhood. But more importantly I loved as it is possible only once in one's life, with all the innocence of my years, with all the hope and pride of adolescence. Two years later Anna sent me an edition of *Manon Lescaut*. But even that story of devotion had no proximity to the quality of allegiance I found with Anna – it seemed mannered and intentionally tragic. Nothing, nothing in the world could convince me my life had not been created for this single, infinite affection.

4

At least, this is said with hindsight. At the time I felt I had no claim on the future at all, only this ecstatic sense of present, of being so totally in love it drew together every atom of my infancy and boyhood; also it promised a mystery I was never really to solve. Our journey to Spain was in a sense just the backcloth to a personal journey of discovery.

We left Munich one summer afternoon. Anna intended to stay in Paris for a year at the end of our trip, so the back of the car was piled high with trunks and suitcases. We drove south to Lake

Constance, dipped into Austria for a night, then made our way across through Freiburg to the Vosges. The weather was fine, but we had no camping equipment and had to spend the first night in a pension above an inn. They only had a double room left, and I took it as all the previous places we had tried were full.

'Are you married?' the chambermaid asked as we went up the narrow pinewood staircase.

'Well, actually, we're not married,' I lied, 'but we are engaged.'

Anna seemed distressed when I came out to tell her; and in the parlour drank a stein of beer, which normally she shunned, as though trying to ease her sadness. But the room was long and thin, and the two single beds were end to end. We undressed in the dark and got into bed, and held hands around the headboard. She seemed calmer, happier then, knowing I was truly in love with her and not simply out for a cheap affair.

The days passed; at nights we slept in double beds and it became harder to resist. But I'd lived with my French girlfriend for four weeks like that and never regretted a moment; there was no hurry. We got to Gerardmer in the Vosges where we stayed with friends of mine from Paris; Anna had to stay the first night in a very expensive hotel, the remaining two nights in a private house.

But nothing could hide or stem our growing physical need of one another; we agreed as soon as we left Gerardmer to make love at last.

And so it was. A simple room in a tedious town on the road to Paris, a double bed, and Anna in her yellow cotton nightdress which barely came down to her thighs, and little yellow briefs. We were both terribly excited and frightened and Anna asked if I had ever done it before and I said yes though I never had and she guided me in and I knew nothing about satisfying, stimulating a woman, knew nothing whatsoever about the sexual act except that I loved Anna with all my heart and soul and we made love all that night.

In Paris we left some of the baggage and hired a tent. Slowly we drove south through the Loire valley, through the Dordogne, and then stayed with some friends of my parents on the coast below Bordeaux. I was alarmed and hurt by Anna's virtual disowning of me before these friends, and cried bitterly. They knew we were in love and were travelling together. Nobody asked Anna to fake detachment from me. A small, leather-faced English house-guest made complimentary asides to Anna while ignoring me, and this made it still worse. I longed to get away after a few days so that we could be on our own. At the risk of being rude I insisted we leave.

Perhaps in similar circumstances, visiting the relations or friends of a much younger girlfriend, I would have acted with similar 'decorum'. But in Anna's disavowal I felt only a kind of betrayal, a lack of courage, and I was wild with resentment and hurt pride. I wanted Anna to love me as completely as I loved her, so completely that nothing else mattered, least of all the moral considerations of others. I had no idea of what I had opened in Anna – or of the abyss to which I had delivered her.

In the meantime the weather was sunny, we pitched our tent wherever we stopped in the dark and woke to unexpected views of mountains, the sea; the one morning the walled city of Carcassonne. The caves of Altamira, the valley of Roncesvalles, a bullfight at Palencia, Toledo, Burgos, Santillana del Mare, villagers threshing corn with oxen and sleds. Every few nights we would take a room in a hotel or pension to clean up, generally eating one meal a day in a restaurant. I could scarcely credit why this beautiful and intelligent woman should have chosen me; as Paris drew closer on the homeward journey I spent hours in tears of apprehension. It meant surrendering the first woman I had ever come to love heart and soul, body and mind; and for what? The future seemed only a cruel trick. I was eighteen: but had I had the strength of mind and character I would have given up my place at Cambridge, which at bottom reflected only my father's expectations, and lived with Anna, studying perhaps in Paris.

It was there, though, that our age difference told. I was too young; and had triggered off a chain of inexorable fears in Anna. I left her at the station, the Gare du Nord, and I cried like a child as the engine pulled out. Everything told me to stay – save reason.

I returned home. The weeks went past, and I received only two letters, composed of a strange mixture of detachment, of delicately guarded affection and mounting despair. By the beginning of October, when I went up to Cambridge, Anna was convinced she was pregnant.

Dear David,

In the past few days I have suffered a breakdown, which might be the cause or result of pregnancy symptoms. I have set reason against feeling, feeling against reason and every shade in between. The conclusion is as follows: It is of no importance whether it is a case of autosuggestion, whether or what form of cunning my unconscious is employing, whether abortions are state-aided in Japan.

Whether I love you because or so that you become the father of a child is not as important as the realization that if I play off father against child or child against father and keep one from the other, love will break down, or rather, I shall break love into pieces . . .

This means: I opt for total love, for the total person, and I turn my consciousness then to the decision and not to the consequences, which do not depend on me. I can make further decisions according to the circumstances.

I await your decision now.

Anna

A few days later, just after the family with whom she was staying had left for a week-end in the country, Anna cut her wrists. However, Madame Libane forgot something in the flat, and insisted her husband return to fetch it. Perhaps a sixth sense told him to check Anna's room, or perhaps he was merely being polite. At any rate he crossed the courtyard and checked Anna's door. He found her unconscious and phoned for an ambulance. At hospital Anna's life was saved, after which she was transferred to the psychiatric wing. It was from there that she wrote to me on 20 October, almost three weeks after her previous letter. She said nothing of the suicide attempt; merely that she had been ill, remembered little of what had happened, and could concentrate only with difficulty because she was on tranquillizers.

I had never in my life encountered a real nervous breakdown, and it was not until January of the following year that I found out what had happened. The weeks of silence before I heard from

Anna in hospital were frightful, and I understood little or nothing of her initial letter. I had stayed with the General, before going up to Cambridge, and to Anna had tried to conceal my personal distress at our separation with letters of confidence and purpose.

I kept up this façade until we met after Christmas in Paris.

She was waiting at the station: and I knew I could never love any other mortal as I did her, never feel such complete tenderness. It was as though I had no self when I was with her, but could only respond to the extraordinary and profound waves of goodness and sensitivity and intelligence which radiated from her. Her eyes were so warm and clever and instinctive, like a shy, wonderful animal – whereas beneath the light, almost pointed nose her mouth told such physical, sensuous stories of delicacy and love. She was three or four inches shorter than I, with the figure of a model. She had high cheek-bones, little ears. I felt she needed someone far older and more firm in character than me – yet that no one could be more aware, more sensitive to her utter femininity, her strange tension between intelligence and sexuality, beauty and shyness.

We bought two rings and became secretly engaged. I should have married her then or at least remained with her, given up my Cambridge course – for she was far too frightened to come with me. I stood walled by the puritanism and propriety of my background on the one side, and my helpless adolescent devotion to Anna on the other. In the very truest sense of the word our relationship was fatal. If I made Anna promise never, never to try to take her life again, if for another ten years she kept her word, it was somehow only a reprieve. In time she would be labelled by doctors using every conceivable category of mental illness – from simple neurotic to incurable schizophrenic. Not until after the final disaster did I learn of the history of mental disorder in her family, on both her mother's and her father's side. Nor did I wish to know – and nor did it prove anything beyond the genetic frailty of a family given to extremes of intelligence and sensitivity. For me she was and would remain utterly, utterly unique. I loved her so deeply I was driven to near insanity, and the years that followed were far from happy in an everyday sense.

I returned to England and to Cambridge: I could barely concentrate. I was childishly ecstatic over our engagement, underwent a period of great introspection and despair amidst the pressure and excitement of university life. Again Anna believed she might be pregnant; I managed to persuade her to come to England at Easter, and my parents to support me if I got married. But she was not pregnant, and the week she spent in England went wrong. The tension at home was unbearable.

A pattern of dependencies, fears, and tensions was thus established within the first year of our love. It would have needed two persons of exceptional robustness to break it and impose something better. Neither Anna nor I was that. The history of my career at Cambridge was erratic. One year I almost failed my Tripos examinations, and came away with a lucky Third; the next I narrowly missed a First. I switched faculties to read History. I would leave Cambridge in mid-term to visit Anna in Paris or later in Munich. I travelled and had fleeting relationships with girls across two continents and loved none but Anna, and was then brokenhearted when she slept with a colleague in her literary seminar at Munich: Christoph.

Time after time Anna's breakdowns recurred in Germany, and her years of study came no nearer termination. The competitiveness and pressure of work were intolerable for her; she seemed to have no way of seeing beyond or outside it, with all her intelligence, as though hypnotized by the complex and reactionary machinery of German academic science. She was reading for a doctorate; it became evident she had not the stamina or psychic physique to withstand the stress. I left Cambridge with a middling degree, quite unsure now whether to do historical research or follow my childhood ambition to 'become a writer'. I spent the summer at home not deciding, and finally accepted a post as factotum with a London publisher. Eight weeks later I resigned; was persuaded to stay on and managed a further month. Finally, in December 1965 I left for good. I took the train to Munich, obtained a job at the Berlitz school. Requiring a work permit from London, Anna and I decided to come back to England. I had obtained for her the chance of a translation of a novel for a Munich publishing house; on the strength of this we got married in London and Anna temporarily gave up her studies. We took a pokey single room, then moved to a flat which we were given free in return for three hours' housework a day. I became a teacher in the ILEA, first in a primary school, then in a boys' grammar. I found the same almost adolescent inability to get on with superiors; I resigned again, and we opened a shop.

This time fate smiled. Our business prospered, Anna finished her translation, and became pregnant. Against medical advice from her doctor and the local psychiatric consultant we decided to have the child, whose intentional conception would have been impossible for us at that moment in our lives.

Thus Gabriel was born. I had to fight my way through to the delivery room to be with Anna because of a recalcitrant obstetrician; but I stood by her, held her hand, gave gas and air, and cried with her pain. From wild-eyed innocent adolescence I had become a shop-owner and a father; and from shy, perennial studentship Anna had graduated to a mother. It was our first major, concrete step in growing up.

Yet this is to mythologize. Although the translation, the shop, and Gabriel's birth provided challenges we met, there were so many we didn't. I expected Anna to conform to a minimum role of housewife, domestically and emotionally. I was both terrified of losing her (as I had always been, inside), and also frustrated by my very dependence on her, my own inability to grow up as a human being. My insistence on material independence, the shop, and later on my writing, was in a sense a substitute for an independence I felt I could not, would never, achieve in the heart. I was faced with the dilemma of wanting to keep Anna, yet knowing she was beyond me. Our life fell into a kind of frail balance. And it was not long before it shattered.

5

We went to the Post Office and looked through the register of medical practitioners. Because his name sounded German we chose Dr D.

When Anna became distraught towards the end of her translation, Dr D. called in the psychiatric consultant from the local hospital. He gave her some tranquillizers and she became an outpatient, visiting him once every few weeks. Then in October 1966, in the same month that we opened the shop, Anna told me she thought she was pregnant.

Dr D. seemed unsympathetic when she told him. Even if she was pregnant, he said to her, it did not matter and could be terminated without difficulty, given her psychiatric history. He did arrange for a urine test, however; and it proved positive.

Now the fireworks began. I had no illusions about the difficulties which a baby would impose: at twenty-two and still a novice in the 'outside' world I could never have taken the decision to have a child myself: I had no confidence in a society which seemed frightening and hostile. But once the prospect became fact I felt adamant Anna should have the child, despite Dr D.'s strong objections.

For three months Anna saw no doctor while the baby inside her grew. At length we registered with another doctor.

But the damage was done. Six weeks after Gabriel was born Anna had a breakdown. She became more and more excited, unable to concentrate on anything but the rising tide of dissatisfaction within her: resentment against her mother, my parents ... She could no longer cope with Gabriel, and I took him up to some friends in Cambridge. Anna's mood seemed to reach a crescendo; finally I was able to get her seen again by the hospital psychiatrist. He told me she would have to be admitted to hospital. I knew she feared electro-convulsive treatment and asked if he proposed to use it. He said he did not inquire how I ran my shop, and that he hoped I trusted him to use the best treatment possible. I asked what would happen if I didn't agree to Anna's hospitalization. He replied he would have her committed. What else could I do?

Reluctantly I gave permission, and my friend Peter drove us to the hospital where she was to stay. Nothing was said on the journey, Anna withdrew into a world of complete silence now, wouldn't give her name when asked, and wrote her maiden name on the form they handed to her. I was terribly upset.

When I visited her the next Monday, she wore an old pink dressing-gown which she held tightly wrapped around her. Her eyes blazed, and she took me by the arm and steered me outside, away from the other women in the ward. There was something urgent and compulsive about her actions. She told me of the occupational therapy session that they had had that morning, with a big dial and the questions. Who was this man, the therapist had asked, pointing the dial to a picture of Hitler. Anna laughed: 'They won't get me that way!'

Anna's conviction that there was a conspiracy to make her talk, and thereby incriminate her, was unshakable, and she begged me not to speak to any of the staff. She believed that a secret service was trying to 'get' her in order to frame my father. When I protested that I would bring my father to see her, if she wished me to prove it wasn't so, she put her hand over my mouth. 'Oh, don't say those things!' she begged me. It was a weird phantasy world – and yet profoundly moving because it was so obviously real to Anna.

For days she clutched my arm and whispered about a conspiracy to torture her for being German, for crimes against the Jews. Then the ECT seemed to take effect, and miraculously within days she was better, lost her distrust of doctors, nurses – even friends I once brought with me. She came out after barely nine days. She was put on a régime of tranquillizers and anti-depressants; they had a mildly doping effect. I fetched Gabriel home and we began again.

A year later, in the same early summer warmth, Anna again broke down. This time I was prepared, and she was allowed to stay in a separate hostel away from the main hospital, without being given ECT. She stayed only a week before she felt able to cope again.

Yet the breakdowns themselves were but the final eruptions of a mind, a personality distraught and unhappy. From the night of our wedding our sexual relationship had changed from ecstatic mutual arousal to a kind of prison of expectations and unwillingness. Something in Anna blocked off. In a way she hated being

112

married, domesticated, in a foreign country – and her way of registering this was by shutting sex into a corner. Instead of examining the causes of this, or insisting on more adequate psychoanalytical help (which I could not afford, but for which I could have borrowed the money), I pocketed my shame and disappointment, and threw everything into first my teaching, then the shop; into Gabriel, into a growing urge to write; and into an extramarital relationship.

Meanwhile Anna, bereft of the kind of moral support that I had provided, however badly, faced with something she had always feared – that I would one day abandon her for another woman – simply found it impossible, alone, to get over her mounting despair. Once again she went mad – though this time in more dramatic terms than she had ever done since the time in Paris, seven years before. She wouldn't consent to go into hospital until I came back from Crete where I had gone for three weeks. Frantic cables were sent to the tiny village on the deserted south coast where I was staying. And when I arrived back in England I found her in my parents' flat brandishing a knife in the kitchen: and assuring me it would be 'better' to take Gabriel's life, to 'spare' him what was coming...

6

It was drizzling as we arrived at the mental hospital. 'Old women everywhere, depressing to bring my young wife there,' I noted later in my diary. 'Her face so drawn, the skin dry, lips cracked and bleeding, body taut.'

I had slept the previous night in the airport lounge at Athens, waiting for the first plane to London – a huge Olympic Boeing carrying only six passengers. Crete had been so beautiful, like living in the imagery of a poem – but I should never have stayed so long. At tea that first day the colour came back a little to Anna's cheeks – 'that softness in her skin, that gentleness that once made the tears well in my eyes'.

But the next day the impact of my return had worn off, and

Anna felt completely abandoned. 'Gabriel! Gabriel!' she called out hysterically.

'He's all right,' I assured her.

'You lie, you lie,' Anna kept moaning, and I could only stand rooted where I was.

'You belong to Helen,' she insisted.

Saturday, 7 June 1969

'3 p.m. visited Anna – pleased to see me I think but the staff had stopped her smoking and she was very nervous. We sat not saying anything, though at first there was hostility in her eyes and she kept miming Gabriel's little actions, like biting his fingers and shaking them, pretending it hurt. The tension of sitting with Anna became terribly exhausting – at the end of two hours I could hardly keep my eyes open.

'At 5 tea was served and I went outside and slept on the grass for nearly an hour.

'When I returned Anna was upset again. In the lounge one of the visitors was hammering away at the piano. We sat again in the drawing-room, but Anna grew upset; a woman gave her a cigarette, and when Anna had smoked it to the filter she wouldn't put it out. I made her. But then she slid around the lino floor, cringing against it with curled body as though she felt more secure so. The woman who had given her the cigarette kept saying: "Anna, get up! Anna get up! Naughty girl!" – and her husband saying "You'll get dirty like that," which was significant. She calmed down a little and we sat together again.

'Tea was served again at 7 p.m., but then suddenly Anna became hysterical, shouting Gabriel's names (Gabriel, Gabe, Gabby) and waving limp arms with a terrifying face of anguish. "Gabriel is all right," I tried to tell her. At first, however, she wouldn't listen and I could hear the other man saying, "Well, at least you can be grateful you're not that bad!" I tried again, explaining that I was her husband. "*Mann*" – she kept turning the word over as though she couldn't believe it. And I said yes, her husband and Gabriel's father; she his mother, my wife. This calmed her down a little; but every so often she would lick her lips

114

with a pointed tongue circulating her jaw as though she were trying to come to terms with something, shuffling her feet too in circles. And then she began singing:

> *Ich hatte einen Onkel*
> *er hiess Max Schreiber*

> [I had an uncle
> who was called Max Schreiber]

in a curious high-pitched witch's voice, ending: "all right?" with a mocking smile (I had asked yesterday whether it was true, as another patient had said, that she had been singing). Suddenly she went on:

> *Und er schrieb einen lebendigen Stil*
> [And he wrote in a lively style]

adding it through clenched teeth, harshly.

' "So do I," I said stupidly – and she burst out hatefully: "*Ja, Du bist ein Dichter* [Yes, you are a writer]" – the word Dichter drawn out with mockery and the hard steel of jealousy so that I felt ashamed of myself – "*und ich bin nicht* creative, not grateful . . ." She was searching for the derogatory terms I perhaps have used to defeat her, and I pined . . .

'Seven-thirty came and the other visitors began to go. I kissed her on both cheeks and the forehead. Her skin so soft. Then the tears welled again to my eyes, the distress of seeing Anna in such a condition, I so helpless to help except by being there. I cried and cried and she held me tight, licking away my tears with her tongue, drying them. "My love, my love," I could only say, holding her tiny waist, her little body which warmly tucks into me as no one else's ever, my love. And we looked at each other through the glass of the door almost as in a film . . .'

Monday, 9 June 1969, 4.45 p.m.

'Anna curiously awake and aware, lively and stimulating. We went for a walk outside and I felt so enchanted by her talking. She was often very funny – for instance she had a fear she would

115

be put down a padlocked coal-chute, or minced in the kitchen mincing-machine, and the smell from the grass bonfire worried her. I said, it's all right, I've been over there, it's definitely grass, I peed on it. Anna looked shocked – as though it was something sacrilegious I had done (actually I'd only done it against a tree nearby). "Do you think that's what they'll do to me?" she asked; and then reflectively: "The Princess and the Pea."

'She was adamant that there was a conspiracy at the hospital (both her doctors were Jewish), and constantly wanted me to reassure her that she would be able to come out alive. And occasionally she would say "I do love you David" – emphatically as though she wanted to believe it. She still imagined I was married to Helen; was sure her mother had died, and Berthold too; and when I asked her how she knew she said by telepathy! Everything she said was so clear, so lucid, and it was only at the corners of things that I realized how ill she still is.'

Tuesday, 10 June 1969

'Drew up in the car, Anna walking in the shade of the trees. She looked up and stared at me disconcertedly as the car stopped. I was married to Helen, wasn't I? She looked very thin and gaunt, tall in her slender long pink dressing-gown without belt and her bag hanging from her shoulder. She would never come out of the hospital, would she? She would stay there for the rest of her life, wouldn't she?

'I showed her what I had bought – knitting needles and wool. Oh yes, she would so much like to knit for Gabriel. I suggested for the child of a friend; she agreed less readily. Let her have Gabriel – *please*, she begged me, and it was so hard to say no. We began to walk a bit and then sit in the sun; she told me her fears again – how the psychiatrist had asked about her three children – she spoke of my mother and of her grandfather who was a Nazi, and how she would have to atone for all the sins of the Germans. Then gradually in the course of that single afternoon she began to get better and told me the course of events that had led up to the breakdown – her refusal to go to my parents' country house, the visit of her brother Berthold and

116

his wife, going to a friend, with Gabriel, to ask her to get in touch with R. D. Laing ... And she quoted so freely from the books she had read – the fairy-tales and novels, thought of the cover of *Dr Faustus* even, which I could not remember.

'And beside this wonderful human being, so full of intelligence and depth, of feeling and anxiety, I felt but a very superficial thing.'

7

However, the days went by and Anna responded so badly to the electro-convulsive therapy (twice a week) that I asked that it be stopped; and in the end discharged her from hospital myself – 'against medical advice'.

Though I did my best to help Anna settle down at home, it wasn't easy. When she questioned herself, lost all faith and courage, I felt as though the bottom was falling out of my world. It was now seven years since I had first met Anna; I was twenty-five. That summer I asked Ted Grant if he could help. After months of waiting Anna was offered a course of psychotherapy at his hospital with a young Canadian doctor.

It was the first time Anna was able to set up a real relationship with a psychiatrist she trusted and could see regularly, who offered reason, not simply drugs and sympathy. She not only 'transferred' love to him; she soon fell deeply in love. Given a domestic situation in which she felt herself an inadequate mother to Gabriel, in which her husband was either writing or running the shop or enjoying the company of another woman, in which she was herself shy and had few or no friends, in which she felt the oppressions of her mother and parents-in-law, and in which she had always to compromise with the customs and environment of a foreign country, it was perhaps no more than logical. I considered her psychotherapy to be her own affair, and asked for no involvement – it never occurred to me that I, or at least our marital relationship, might be the cause or trigger to her psychological distress. I both treated her as 'patient' and yet refused to act either doctor or nurse. I felt that underneath I loved her unequivocally, and that this was enough.

But as Anna grew more and more deeply attached to her psychiatrist, a relationship of my own with a new woman, the wife of a friend who lived nearby, became serious. What had begun, on my part, as something light suddenly altered shape and colour; our love affair took her breath away, and she gave herself to me like a schoolgirl, with total innocence, total trust. She was English, she had a face of shattering, cool beauty. To touch her was to feel alive in my most poetic, masculine self. 'I can't help loving you physically too,' she wrote to me in the summer of 1969. 'When I see you in public I am frosty and embarrassed because to touch you is exquisite, you have only to lean across me to "tidy" things for me to have to move away before I caress you. I don't dare smile at you because I couldn't stop if I started.

'David, I love you. And I can be happy doing this within the necessary confines of our situation. You have added another dimension to my life – cliché tho' that is.'

Though I forbade her to speak of Anna, she made it clear she felt Anna was chaining, paralysing me. It did not occur to me that I was doing the same to Anna.

My diary became a record of growing despair. I knew I still loved Anna, that nothing could separate us if we wanted to make our love work; but the continual pattern of depression, of moody introspection, the obsession with problems of self exasperated me, while her increasing emotional attachment to her new therapist meant that our physical love-making and tenderness became less frequent and less satisfactory.

I began to see in Juliette a sort of god-given angel who might rescue me – though she herself, wounded by my early unserious-ness and then confused by my deepening expectations, did not. I went away to Switzerland by myself, but it didn't really help. I asked Juliette if she would marry me – both as a test of my own earnestness and a test of her. I felt I must break the web that tied me: but it was internal, not external, and no outward change could help.

I still saw both Helen and Juliette; but whether as a result of her therapy or not Anna now pressed that we should have another child. Juliette said it would inevitably mean the end of our relationship. I was unhappy and resisted. Nevertheless Anna became pregnant, and once again the matter became a *fait accompli*.

This time Anna had no fear. The baby, a boy, was born at home, in the house we had bought near the park and our shop, in our own room, our own setting.

The pregnancy and birth seemed to change Anna. That year – 1970 – she suffered no breakdown; nor did one come post-natally. My affair with Juliette came to an end. Anna's psychotherapist returned to Canada, and she declined the offer of an alternative therapist. The psychotherapist had proved she could overcome her anxieties and depressions without recourse to madness. She now wanted her own therapist – but this time outside the National Health Service, outside the system entirely. She wanted Laing.

8

16.7.71

Dear R. D. Laing,

You saw me for an 'initial consultation' in 1969 (late April or early May); you may still have my first letter somewhere in your files. You were to suggest a doctor for therapy. It did not come to that, I had a breakdown afterwards and then lost contact.

Anyway, here I am two years later, asking for another consultation. Obviously anything I write will seem arbitrary; why mention this aspect and not that – yet I will try to give a short summary of things as I see them at this moment. I have had half a dozen breakdowns, and have had a year's 'analytical therapy' which broke the pattern of breaking down, but leaves me on pills. More therapy has been suggested to conquer my 'excessive jealousy' of my husband, his former mistress and his work (writing). But I do not want to be a 'patient' any longer, and if I have therapy I am going to pay for it (I can earn money by translating, being German). Because what I need is outside guidance to establish a new pattern of interpersonal relationships, as one tends half consciously to compensate for all deliberate steps one takes to alter a situation. For it will upset the family balance, my husband won't like it, but I want to be a (creative) person in my own right and not sub-servient and underneath 'trying to get my own back', that is, make them pay, after all, for the support I give to them. I hate the whole set-up, and I want to get out of it ...

My brother had made 'discreet' inquiries about Laing after Anna's 1969 breakdown, and about his place outside London where schizophrenics could act out their psychoses without ECT or drugs. He had reported negatively – and Anna's letter to Laing must have required considerable courage. In the summer of 1971 she set down her feelings about conventional medicine, the way she had hitherto been treated by doctors and psychiatrists, as follows:

You were responsible for making me go bad, go rotten; then, well prepared with new bones, tablets and prescriptions you set the robot on the rails which suited you. The robot's language was parrot-talk, not dangerous, childish. That is how you wanted me, and you stopped at nothing, not even force. Military doctor and psychiatrist – even the hospital chaplain: it was a perfect alliance. I went as a mummy amongst you, only vaguely registered your shadows, the shadows you throw and the shadows that are your flesh. My X-ray eyes didn't appeal to you, my hands had to be occupied with sewing. You prescribed evening courses to keep my brain cells active, and one of you even wanted to take my child from me. Do you think I can ever forget that? Do you think there can ever be good excuses for that? The next tablets you hand out you must swallow yourselves. Bread and watery soup for the arrogant doctor in the white coat; but this time, this one time it must be prison, not the madhouse. R. D. Laing would have let me write, or ought to have done had he not fallen into Zen Buddhism and God knows what else. Stephen did not think his asylum for artists the right place for me. At bottom only the frustration of an academic at home, domesticized, not a question of creativity. Just because I don't paint. If the boy imagines he's found womanly perfection in his own wife, he's made a mistake. They could have saved me years of side-turnings, but R. D. Laing didn't belong to a proper hospital, was suspect. You all have an unspoken interest in keeping me a half-idiot, a not-quite-accepted member of the family, each out of fear of what I see through – the part he is trying to kill off in himself or at least will not admit to.

My own stupid mother wanted me weak so that she could spend her whole life making good again. Thank you. But you are far worse. You want me mad, so that you don't have to be ashamed.

Laing suggested his colleague Roy Landis; and on 10 September 1971 at 9.30 a.m. Anna began her very first own-chosen therapy.

'Reason for coming' she headed some notes before she left that day in September:

1. Fed up with being patient, ill and weak. 2. Disbelief in theories which relate everything to childhood trauma (rejecting mother – loss of father). 3. Need to blame my husband and his inadequacy (it was not treason of my father that was the reason of my first breakdown, but awareness of basic unreliability in my then boyfriend).

She wanted to find and to assert a real self, to be without shame or inhibition. She wanted an existentialist therapist who would acknowledge that the fault was not only in herself, but in the world. A part of her doubted even whether therapy was necessary if only she could get me to understand what was happening, to stop defending myself so self-righteously. On her thirty-fourth birthday, in September 1971, she drafted a letter (which was never in fact given to me) which began:

Dear David,
  If you were really prepared to take on responsibility I might not need all this therapeutic counselling.
  But deep down you are not, however much you try to be a 'good father'. You hide in your work, your fiction, your poetic theories. I admit you have been deeply wounded by the disappearance of passion which you, a dreamer, need. What would be left, once your dreams and your rhetoric go? It will not be me who gets you out of your world, but one day you will have to leave it. All I can do is be prepared for that day. I am neurotic, hysteric, schizoid, so I will seek 'treatment', but I have to go about it in my own way ...

And to a friend of ours who had moved away from the neighbourhood:

Dear Sally,
  I feel like slowly exploding, and you are the only one I can write to. David has come home from the shop with a whole host full of tales. First a poet, who usually lives in Italy, asked him for a drink; that was at lunchtime. Two hours later Helen rang David up to ask whether he knew where this poet who stays in her house (she has left her husband) could possibly be, and at the same time asking David what she could

do – he gets drunk every day, lives on her money, etc. Well, David feels he can't do much, it is her problem; I suppose, just as he tended to say to me that he could not do much about his parents, that was my problem; anyway this may be off the point. This poet told him about Ted Hughes, his first wife, Sylvia Plath, who wrote *The Bell Jar* and committed suicide, and then he married again and his second wife committed suicide, killing her child with her. I suppose this sequence is really what made me sick, and the poet's explanation: 'Certain men attract unstable women.' And then hear David on the telephone to his designer-friend about the layout of a poem which David's friend, a poet, has written, who was himself an alcoholic for ten years; David's voice, tense and intense, as it only gets about matters of 'ART' – and to realize suddenly, abruptly, that I am myself bloody well responsible for my own saneness, in spite of David's so-called novels, and the fact that living with him could drive quite a few women mad. I wonder to what extent Art thrives on the madness of our society, and from where 'artists' take the right to inflict on other people the consequences of their own obsessions. And I see that insane behaviour is not much more than a negative reflection of this our insane society; one form of madness provoking the other. The other being the clinical one, which in itself is not capable of any constructive approach, though mad people may be quite talented, often above the average. Does all this make sense to you?

At last Anna had found the courage to question her environment, the established order of things – to turn the tables on her 'oppressors' as she called them. But the oppressors still held the power – and Anna couldn't change that, Laing couldn't change it. Not unless she could first change me, that is.

As the pain and shame of my love affair with Juliette receded, our marriage began to alter. Unwilling at first to have a second child I now found I loved Thomas no less than I did Gabriel. I wrote out my relationship with Juliette in a novel.

'"Is Elizabeth your tiger?" the wife asks in his novel,' Anna noted after reading parts of it surreptitiously in manuscript. 'And to see how he re-hashes the end, his position towards his wife, rehearsed over and over again – you will never get that ending right, Elizabeth did not die! It is me who will die of cancer, and not of the cervix, but of the lungs! Fags, consumed in spite of you, and these notes written in spite of you. Oh yes, only you can write

122

and bring the tears to my eyes, and you may be very perceptive. But this you will not find, my sketches and my hate . . .'

'I should have scratched her face, her pretty cheeky face, scarred forever,' Anna wrote in a piece she called *What I Should Have Done*. 'David as usual, standing by, watching the women fight it out, and when I had lost, then be generous . . . Well Roger [Juliette's husband] won in the end, I won in the end – the truth is, you have to win here and now I'm afraid.'

Anna did 'win' over Juliette – but how transform that victory into peace, into a marriage that be viable, worthwhile, by choice and not history?

I decided I ought to finish running the shop and go abroad for a while – a sort of sabbatical year in which I might explore a new relationship with Anna. I suggested Germany as it would give Anna a chance to speak her own tongue again, and because of its associations. Anna preferred Austria – she loathed the regimentation that had characterized her upbringing and youth, however deeply imbued she might be with German language and literature. It seemed a happy compromise.

However, the shop wasn't sufficiently profitable to pay for the trip. I would have to earn money. Hence came the idea for a book to be written by us both, a story of brotherhood, telling the life stories of two of the most important twentieth-century men of letters.

Once again it was an opportunity for us to work together – the more so because so many of the themes of the story were reflected not only in modern history, but in ourselves, in our own relationship. Anna's natural sympathy was for the older protagonist, the forgotten, less successful, more bohemian brother, with his epigrammatic wit, his fiery style, his concern with human responsibility; whereas my response was primarily to the younger, egocentric but more artistically perfect brother.

Dear David,

This book is a unique chance for both of us, and we must not destroy it. I said once you got going you would knock me into the ground, and you are about to do it. You get so engrossed in yourself when you work hard – ruthless, regardless of the victims. Can't you see this book as a chance to get over your own ruthlessness? What helps you all the insight of the world, if it is only your insight and does not take into account my experience? You must see that it is not good for anyone always to get things his own way – you create resentment which in the end acts as a saboteur. Why do I have to tell you all this? Should you now know without me? You do know, so why do you choose to forget?

I did know (though Anna never gave me the letter) ... I knew it was important to her to participate fully in the venture, and at first Anna did extensive research with me, concentrating mainly on the elder of the two brothers. We had many long discussions and arguments, as we went over our findings. But Anna had an axe to grind: her purpose was to reinstate the elder, politically oriented brother against the younger one, who had been the subject of so much of her own university work. I agreed with many of her feelings – but we weren't setting out to write a defence of Anna's own political views, I felt. First and foremost we had a story to tell, the remarkable story of a unique relationship, with its symbolic strains and the gradual development in it of tolera-tion, understanding, and reconciliation. 'David, as usual, standing by . . .'?

I don't know. I did my best not to 'knock' Anna 'into the ground'. Because of her new therapy with Dr Landis in Septem-ber 1971 we abandoned our plan to go to Vienna for a year, and I did my continental research in three visits to France, Germany, and Switzerland the following year. I was ruthless with myself and only worked in the mornings. If I had not found sufficient wisdom to collaborate with Anna on the actual manuscript – saw it too clearly as a human, epic story neither intrinsically critical nor academic – I did at least begin to approach maturity by my very grapplings with the theme – the nature of human growth, of courage, of forgiveness and concilia-tion without loss of contact with truth. I was overwhelmed by this realization. It impregnated everything I wrote, everything I felt, everything I saw. The two years I spent working were without doubt the happiest and most rewarding of my life – and of my marriage.

For Anna it was not the same. She had the distress of watching while the book slipped into my domain and out of her grasp, even though her work on the subject promised to make a book in its own right, and gave her tremendous intellectual stimulation. She filled notebook after notebook with jottings. She wrote reams of poetry, miniature autobiographical tales, and extensive critiques of other books – on sociology, psychology, education, and anthropology – which she had read. Together with this she continued a twice-weekly analytical and existential psychotherapy and coped with two small children (albeit with the help now of a Finnish au pair).

In May 1972 Anna wrote to me:

I like to have things straight – what is wrong with that? What is wrong with anything? What is wrong with me? I know I've a history of 'breakdowns' – had they at the first incident given me different treatment, in a different place, it all might not have happened over and over again. And even if – I don't have 'breakdowns' now – with or without the inverted commas. I get furious, excited, depressed – why not? Nothing will be better in two or three years' time, at the distant end of therapy. Maybe it would be, objectively, but in the meantime I've got to live. Live.

I walked out of the therapy session today. Of course I will go back, but not with the same frequency, nor in the same attitude – as if everything about me was wrong and needed correcting. I feel quite normal, thank you very much. By which I don't mean to get at you. At heart myself, and my projections onto the analyst.

Of course there seems to be a pattern – that I throw things up when you are away. Necessary perhaps, definitely necessary.

I went to Fulham Broadway Tube Station, walked all the way along Fulham Road to find a shop with certain clothes I had in mind, saw a beautiful Iraqi rug, really beautiful, if only I knew where to put it. Tried on various clothes and before leaving threw the whole lot I had chosen upon a heap of other tried-on-clobber. I wish I had done that with more of the clothes I ended up with.

Perhaps one should buy what one really likes. Years ago I bought some Batik material – it waited 15 years, and now I can make a skirt from it.

I am fed up with all that symbolic acting out. (There was a radio programme criticizing Laing's something-for-everybody irrationalism.) I am fed up with complications and complexity. I want things straight.

And a few days before that:

Until now I have loaded responsibility for almost everything onto you – shop, car, garden, house, money – and spiritual uplift. Poor man. I started going to an evening class in Zen. A different kind of world. Though I wonder whether it will do me much good. I nearly had a row with Dr Landis – fed up with the passivity he imposes. He says this is primarily sexual; I am more concerned with the wider implications, perhaps after the initial problem has been located. His continuous emphasis on being rather than achieving. Sunday today – no work for you. Or are you writing?

Love, love, love

Anna

She criticized me for not sharing more of the domestic burden with her, and yet acknowledged that there was a whole world she pushed onto me and only recognized when I was away. She wanted to find herself:

I feel I need a long time on my own to learn again who I really am, she had written on 12 May 1972. How can I know what I want when I don't even know who this [I] is? There is too much pressure on us. Each child represents a new world, and the old one, our own, we haven't even conquered. In this sense a woman has it so much harder in knowing what she wants: she lives within traditional structures passed on from mothers and mothers-in-law. To change them requires will-power. But will-power requires an identity and regarding 'I' see above.

She wasn't joking. She was confused by her inability to make progress – but how *could* she do that as long as I clung to my illusions of Art and endeavour – in reality nothing more than a chauvinism which excluded and oppressed her? What use was all my understanding, patience, and consideration if at heart I still pursued a personal objective that was the projection of my need for integrity and wholeness, if this served to fragment the personality of my own wife? When I told her my intention to dedicate the book to my own brothers she burst out: 'You will not. You will dedicate it to me!'

Anna had the sharpest mind of anyone I have ever known. She understood my own 'horror of domesticity' as she put it in her notes, as 'fear of mutilation (castration), fear of being swallowed up' – and I suppose I saw Anna's own burgeoning intellectual

126

creativity as a threat to my own. *Tout vient à temps pour qui peut attendre*, Anna noted at the bottom of the sheet of paper. But could she wait?

The year 1972 came to a close. Three days before Christmas I met Juliette in the street.

Friday Morning

The chance meeting
Seems casual
The words trip pat
From dry lips
Your hair is pulled back
And when you smile
The reality of our separation
Engulfs me.

Here by the park
On the grey pavement
Of everyday life
Old loves touch
Fumble for recognition

Who left whom?
And does it matter?
Love is a bold enterprise
For adventurers
We bid each other farewell
And though you draw away
It is as if
We had drawn closer.

Juliette had recently found an old photograph she had taken of me. Returning to Anna I felt how much that reflected of these two relationships – the one photographic, photogenic, a meeting of light-sensitive beings; while the other was the story of life, of humanity.

My biography was finished on 7 April 1973, soon after my twenty-ninth birthday. My diary records that already in mid-January Anna had been 'near to breakdown'; but with Landis's help she had come through. On 17 March she left with Gabriel for a visit to her brother and her mother – her last visit to Germany.

My publisher was mulling over the synopsis of a book about Crete that I now wished to write; and I felt we ought to go out there *en famille* – both to recuperate and for research.

I felt closer to Anna then than at any other time in our marriage, and proud of my achievement in completing the book, for it went far beyond my own egocentric preoccupations, was written with all the patience and understanding I could command. But for Anna it was different. She had held back, had disciplined herself to support me – had even begun to translate the work in the hope of getting a German publisher; and she had had to repress so much of her own frustration and despair. For three years she had avoided breaking down. Her notebooks began to swell. She would spend hours typing away in her study, trying to come to terms with it all – her self-hate, her hatred of her mother, her past, my own family, me. No one could perceive her own self as Anna could in her moments of precision. In a series of autobiographical critiques and observations Anna now wrote out a long poem. In it she looked at herself with cold, dispassionate eyes. Perhaps, in style, it was modelled on Sylvia Plath, her 'hero' figure. It charted her progress from childhood; from the death of her father to her abortive relationship with Ludwig; the birth of her own children, her impulse to kill Gabriel when she broke down in 1969.

She wanted to clarify, to make it clear.

Structure, the saving structure. If life is a rubbish-heap
Structure it. If you cannot find your feet in life
Structure it. If you criticize yourself and do not know where to turn
Structure yourself.
Structuring is better than cutting arteries,
Structuring is better than the hashish-trip.
Only having children transcends structures; but who can afford to have
More than two children?

In England the nursery schools are better
In Germany one is regimented
In England one is manipulated
From regimentation I slipped to manipulation.

My children tear my insides from my womb
The emotional turmoil
In the evening I am a piece of raw flesh.

Analysis so far

Stage I: wanting to be looked after at Landis's
Stage II: wanting to seduce Landis
Stage III: rejection:
           wanting to stop analysis
           wanting to do my own thing
Stage IV: 'breakdown'
           – wanting to be held
           and regression into infancy

All the time acting out of minor phantasies: long dress, lady, writer
Not so minor in fact: they all revolve around female identity

I would like to break through
to a new honesty
– A new honesty?
Honesty is what we are,
the others are charlatans
said my mother
and I willingly believed it.

   She wrote about everything from her own schizophrenia to penis envy and infantile sexuality, from bombing in Hanover to IRA bombs in London.

   She wanted to break out of an impossible world. Laing, Landis insisted this should be done without incarceration in asylums, without electroshocks, without extensive drugs. Though Anna had latterly become more disenchanted with Laing's existentialist positions (she wrote pages of notes after the broadcast about Laing's 'Something for Everyone' psychiatry), and saw his interest in Zen Buddhism as taking refuge, it was nevertheless Laing's theory of undeterred 'breakthrough' that was adopted once Anna finally went mad.

   My own doubts I saw as crises of moral courage. Though I had loved Anna unequivocally for almost eleven years I felt I must now stand up and be counted, must stand by Anna in a trial which Landis insisted was Anna's own choice. I knew nothing of Anna's writings, knew only that I endorsed her wish

129

to become whole, to live with hope and not anxiety, with pride and not shame. Around me during those six weeks in which Anna acted out her psychosis I heard both admiration and horror. Neither touched me. What I did, what I underwent in those stark, endless days and nights of madness I accepted as a test of faith, of love; and of humanity.

But was this really the way to do it? Why invest such importance in this one event, why court such danger – for Ted Grant warned me what might happen. Could it ever have been worth the prize?

Yet Anna *did* come through – ecstatically, triumphantly, after six long weeks of total insanity. Until the moment I heard her voice coming from the bathroom, soft, gentle, crooning, and I called her to the bedroom.

Part Three
The Trial

1

She stands in the doorway, naked, her hair up in a sort of bun, her skin a dark colour, as though smeared with dirty oil. Her eyes are sunk way back into their sockets.

'Oh Anna,' I sigh. 'What have you done?'

She stands there like a child who has done something silly, as I get out of bed and go over to comfort her. My first thought is that she has rolled herself in the dung in the barn. I am not angry. I want to take her in my arms and say that it doesn't matter. But as I draw closer there is a strange, acrid smell, and behind her on the floor, a trail of bloody footprints that stretches across the hall from the bathroom.

I have a sudden vision of Anna having cut herself deliberately, her womb, which would explain why no blood shows on her skin. I take her arm and lead her quickly to the bathroom, dreading what I shall find – visualizing a bath full of blood. The footprints lead to the bath; but in it there are only strips of grey material floating in clear water. It is now I realize that they are bits of skin, and I look again at Anna. The strange smell is of burned, singed hair; the smears of 'oil' on her body smoked, peeling flesh. She has been burned!

I scream for Satu. My instantaneous reaction is to feel I must lift Anna into the bath.

Then Satu opens her door, and the children look up, awake, and begin to scream. I tell Satu to go back, to look after them until I return.

I throw on some clothes and rush down the staircase with Anna. There is blood on the carpet. I imagine perhaps the barn is ablaze.

But outside is strangely peaceful. The wet grass beside the porch is a lighter green than the rest, and there are cinders. I realize later they must have been Anna's clothes, that she must have rolled out the fire in the wet grass before coming in and turning on the bath.

We have to run up a rather rocky, sharp-stone path to the car, and I dread what that will do to Anna's feet: I tell her to run on the grass verge.

But the windows of the car are dark when I reach it; and when I open the door clouds of black smoke billow out. It will be impossible to take her to hospital in it.

The fire seems to have died down: the cushions on the rear benches are smouldering; the spare red petrol canister stands in the middle of the floor; without a top. This must be where it took place.

I get in and pull the fire extinguisher from its brackets, spray the petrol canister and the benches with the white powdery mixture. Then I tell Anna to wait on the grass while I telephone for an ambulance. I have thrown an Indian cotton dressing-gown over her shoulders: but I have no idea whether this is the right thing to do. I know so little about burns. I can do nothing to relieve her pain if she is suffering. Yet during all these minutes she has never uttered, made a sound but only looked at me with this expression of childlike helplessness, naked and trembling. She squats on the grass and begins to sob – a sort of crooning to herself while I run down the other side of the farmhouse to the back door.

I knock and go straight in. Mrs Brideson is standing there over the stove. I ask if I can phone her doctor, there's been a terrible accident.

She motions to the telephone at the other end of the room. She tells me the name of the doctor to look up in the personal telephone directory beside it. I ask the code, she gives it without moving from the stove, and I dial.

The doctor answers.

I say that my wife has tried to commit suicide and is burned all over. Can he send an ambulance?

Then I ask which hospital Anna will be taken to. He says to the cottage hospital.

I hesitate.

134

'What's the matter with that?' he asks.

I say I know the hospital, have seen it while visiting the village, but wonder whether it is big enough for an emergency case like this.

'Well where would you like her to go?' he retorts.

I say I hardly know the area, have only been there four days. I name the nearest large town I have seen on the map.

'Are you going to argue over where she goes?' he demands; and I have to give in, apologize, appeal to him only to get the ambulance up to the farm as quickly as he can.

I'm right: the little hospital is not in any way equipped for such a case. About fifteen minutes elapse before the ambulance comes, and a further ten while we drive downhill to the village. At the hospital Anna is wheeled into the small dressing-room/theatre; and for the first time I hear her scream wildly as they attempt to dress her wounds, particularly her feet. The doctor gives her a pain-killing injection, and then comes out to me.

We sit in the ante-room, by the main entrance.

He is visibly moved and aware of my own distress. I tell him how we had come down to the country with a number of other schizophrenics under Dr Landis, that I hadn't wanted her to have ECT, that she had apparently emerged from the psychosis: and then the accident happened.

He says he doesn't care for ECT either, that it is very seldom used down there. He doesn't think the burns are deep except on the feet. He is tempted to keep her there, in the cottage hospital, and to dress them himself, as he has done with another patient not long ago. I sigh with relief. I ask how long it will take for the burns to heal sufficiently for Anna to leave: he says three days: but that he is going to have her sent to the nearest town as there is a psychiatric social worker in attendance at the hospital there.

The ambulance driver comes in to telephone. He asks the doctor what percentage of burns he should give. Seventy-five?

The doctor shakes his head. 'No, no. Probably not over fifty.'

The doctor draws out his fountain pen, writes a brief explanatory letter for the casualty officer at the other hospital, then leaves.

Anna is wheeled back into the ambulance. A volunteer nurse has arrived by now and she comes with us, giving Anna constant sips of water on the way. It takes almost an hour. We stop at Patty's cottage and I rush in, shouting for her. I tell her what has happened, ask her to try and get Landis to come to the hospital, as I can't reach him at the other community cottage. She promises, and I run back to the ambulance.

At the hospital Anna is wheeled into the casualty department, and then straight into the small theatre there. The ambulance driver and the nurse leave – he is the local postman in the village he tells me, but the letters will have to be a little late that day – and I sit in the waiting-room among outpatients with bandaged fingers and swollen legs. Later I'm asked by a nurse what's the matter with me, and I explain I'm Anna's husband. She looks a little flustered and says the casualty officer would like a word with me when he has finished in theatre.

He comes out eventually, and asks me to go into his office. He has a serious, methodical face.

His desk is full of forms and sheets of notepaper. He stands facing them, turning the letter from the cottage hospital doctor over in his fingers.

'Do you realize how serious it is?' he asks.

I feel a strange, panicky feeling in my stomach and tell him what the other doctor has assured me, that the burns aren't deep.

He shakes his head.

'It's very difficult to say at this stage how deep the burns are. My guess is that they're all deep –'

'Even on the face?'

'Even on the face. We can't tell for several days – for several weeks in fact. But all burns are serious. It's the shock to the body in the first instance, and the loss of body fluid. We can give her blood and fluid. But you must realize she may die.'

It's the first time the notion of death has occurred to me: my whole body reacts. How can she die when she had been standing before me, when we ran together up the path? She had been singing to herself in the bathroom, loud enough to wake me. No

136

bone was broken and there was only a little blood from the soles of her feet . . .

I step gingerly out and across the corridor, silent. A nurse gives me a cup of tea from a machine in the waiting-room there: then I break down completely as the implications steal through me. A sort of mad internal dialogue seems to overtake my mind as its rational, everyday imagination suddenly leaps into time future, while the rest screams with terror and emotional abandonment.

They clear the room while I sob on the floor, kneeling against my chair in a kind of prayer, begging that it shouldn't happen, that they should save Anna.

2

I'm allowed to go up as soon as Anna is settled in the ward. I can't see the consultant then because he is operating – till six at night.

They have screened off a bed at the end of the ward, a sort of sun terrace which has had to be used to make up for the shortage of beds. Opposite Anna is a child of about nine; but by the afternoon they have cleared the whole four-bed terrace and closed off the casement doors giving access to it.

A short, middle-aged nurse in a special white smock is sitting by Anna: Jane she calls herself.

I have to wear a smock too.

Anna's face looks more peaceful against the white pillow. She is asleep; a series of tubular angle-brackets hold the sheets from actually touching the burned flesh. She seems in no way disfigured and I marvel at how beautiful she looks, even though they have cropped her singed hair closer to her head. Above her hangs the drip-feed.

At lunchtime I go for a walk with Jane; return. Later in the afternoon Dr Landis comes, and we go out for a coffee at a nearby cafe. He is wearing his red anorak. For the first time I feel close to him, almost like a brother, because I'm distressed, and I need him. I see so clearly Landis's own problems, his own attempt at integrity, the pressure he's under every day of his life. I feel him so close I could almost touch him, his almost saintliness.

When we talk of what has happened, Landis develops his own interpretation: the significance of fire, the symbol of clearing, cleansing herself, a kind of resurrection, rebirth, whereas I see it much more as a moment of confusion, depression, as the very pit of despair, of self-hate. Guilt makes me tremble: for not having been able to stop her, for not having realized how serious her state had become. I was with her, I was her guardian, Mary Barnes had warned me: and like Peter I had slept . . .

The important thing now is to see that Anna gets the very best medical attention possible in the best hospital, Landis says. But it seems obvious to me that Anna can't be moved in her present condition. It is a case of helping her, encouraging her to fight.

I ring my father, ask him to find out whether there are any other steps I can take. Should Anna be transferred to another hospital, and if so, to which?

At six finally the consultant comes down: a balding, kindly-faced man in his late fifties or early sixties, stooping slightly. He shakes his head.

'It's very, very grave,' he says quietly behind the screens. 'I don't think she can withstand it. But she's still a young woman. She's got age on her side.'

I sit with Anna all evening. It is arranged that I may sleep on the empty bed in the corner, so that I can go to her if she wakes and wants me. She seems to have no idea where she is or what has happened: only that I'm with her, beside her bed. Her face has begun to swell as though inflated, the flesh around the eyes ballooning, so that her eyes seem long, Burmese.

Stephen arrives at about 1 a.m. He has driven over from the place where he is on holiday with his wife and children.

3

From now on I begin to keep the diary I abandoned when Anna finally 'emerged' from her psychosis at the farm. Though only fragmentary it gives me a feeling at least of continuity, and acts as a kind of escape valve.

If I'm suddenly braked in the struggle for sanity and growth, if in a medical sense I am now superfluous, am condemned to watch while the fight becomes one of medicine against injury, inwardly I feel as though nothing has changed: the circumstances have merely intensified the struggle. Previously we have been fighting for sanity, for a better, more honest marriage, existence; now we are fighting for life.

Anna's trial becomes my own, just as her madness has been.

4

Thursday, 21 June 1973

'Woke about 7. Stephen had not slept – I had heard sound of nurses turning Anna in my sleep, though. She not awake. Face still swollen, and wounds now turning from pale to a garish red where top skin burned or peeled away. Stephen does not want to look.

'Have breakfast. Intend to leave with Stephen to go and see children as Anna asleep and heavily sedated. Wait in car while Stephen tries to phone Bridget. See consultant's car – decide to go up. He is in Anna's room – wait in main ward. After a little while he signals I may come over. Seems very quiet, not willing to say much.

'"Will she live?" I ask.

'He looks at me with his blue eyes that seem to hide in the shyness of his face and bearing. "Oh, she could still pull through. She's done very well to come through the night, very well indeed. Hasn't she?" he says, turning to nurse. Nurse agrees. "We shall have to see in the next 24 hours. But she's getting plenty of plasma and blood and she's not in any pain."

'He departs and I stand by the bed. Suddenly Anna seems to become conscious. Starts talking – about children etc. Seems reassured I am there.

'"Are you going away?" she keeps asking.

'"No, I'll be with you – always." But she gives a little snort at this. Go on talking with her for about $\frac{1}{2}$-hour. Then staff nurse insists I ought to go out a little and see the children, if only for an hour. Leave phone number and go with Stephen. Mary Barnes and American boy in corridor. They ask how Anna is. Just seems so hopeless the moment I am out. When I think of the burns, I burst into tears again.

'In the village I get a garage mechanic to come and check the van for safety; but there is no one at the village police station, so the accident is not reported. At the farm there are the children. How tell them?

'First Thomas comes out with Satu. Roy Landis there too with his small daughter. Says has spoken with Gabriel and told him his mother might die. Mrs Brideson there too. I apologize for it all having happened like this, that Anna might die. She chokes back tears when she says yes, she knows, she is sorry, she was so shocked when it happened, has since been going over and over it all with her husband. Says he had seen her outside before he went to milk cows sometime before 7 a.m. This surprises me – means I must only have dozed very briefly, for I remember Anna going to window in our bedroom when farmer's car left drive; and accident happened circa 7 a.m. "We feel ever, ever so much for you and for her. As the doctor says, we must just pray ... It's very good if you can believe in God ..."'

Stephen remains with the children at the farm, while I return to the town.

5

Friday, 22 June 1973

'Slept 1 a.m.–5 a.m. Woken – Anna calling me. Nurses changing sheets and turning Anna. Sat with her – as lucid as last night – but still thinking *I* have met with accident. Don't know whether to tell her. Say she has had some nasty burns – seems to remember a little – "*ach, ja*". Sipping lot of water – good sign. Face still swollen laterally and mouth/lips enlarged, but colour of face, though still very grey and red where deep burns run (right side behind cheeks), somehow looking better. Wounds on forehead now quite dry. Skin between and below breasts has turned to black, pungent, bad smell of decayed flesh. Only shoulders, front and back, seem to have been spared at all. Below stomach the sight is indescribable – can only think of pictures of babies in foetus stage, a seemingly transparent layer of skin under which the red blood and black network of veins. Horrible, horrible to see. Left leg worse than right. Skin beginning to dry in "waves". Large areas of soles on feet simply come off – but important thing seems to be that all the wounds have now dried. Some areas of superficial skin still hanging tenaciously to legs.

'Says she cannot move fingers. Nurse says seems they are in spasm: but yesterday night nurse had helped her flex them, so I put on gloves and did the same, finger by finger. They are very stiff, no nails, the palm-sides at the fingertips very black and charred – something so naked and infant-like about them – black veins showing in the red and black.

'"You'd have made a very good doctor," Anna murmurs – still very, very lucid, aware of all noises about her, but able only to see a little, eyelids both horribly swollen, almost to the level of cheeks.

'"The children?" she asks. I tell her where they are, of Stephen taking them to the sea, how well Gabriel has taken it ("sharing" me with her as he put it), that they will be asleep at this hour. Seems not to know where she is. Explain about the town, not far from farm.

141

'Very anxious when nurse turns her, wanting me to be there. Heartbeat reasonably steady at 120.

'" *Roy war hier* [was Roy here]?" she asks.

'"Yes," I say, was here last night, that he wants her to live as much as I do.'

How aware Anna is, in a rational sense, of what is happening is difficult to know. She is on constant morphine injections, and the pain must be unbelievable. She speaks repeatedly of 'monsters down there' (hand on her chest). 'That's all right,' I say. 'Oh you're always saying that!' Anna snaps reproachfully: and I have to observe the finest of distinctions between comforting and patronizing. The question, too, of why she did it also rises repeatedly in my mind – but it seems of such tiny importance in comparison with the task of keeping her alive, encouraging her to fight and to live.

6

'"Perhaps better not drink too much," I say when she begins to cough after a number of sips.

'"Oh, a certain amount of drink releases a certain amount of thought," Anna says.

'"Terrible smell," Anna remarks at one point.

I tell her it is the antibiotic spray.

'Seems to have short minutes of rest or sleep, then wakes, calls my name – seems reassured when I answer. If I speak to nurse over screen thinks I am going to leave her. Must have heard of the regional hospital, for asks when I shall be going, as though it would be without her.

'SEN nurse (green) comes to see Anna – one who had advised transfer on first day – surprised how well Anna looks. Says went off duty 2 p.m. yesterday and didn't think she would see her alive again. Only 1 in 150 survive this degree of burns. Felt road journey to the regional hospital too long (4 hours). Senior nursing tutor – a voice like Miranda's – says only her will to live *could* have brought her through to present state.

'Sister asks if she wants porridge – and she takes it from spoon! Unbelievable only 12 or 24 hours before. Then, when asked if any special dish she would like, says fish!'

'I left about 11 a.m. How different from yesterday at the same time! The bloated look, the swollen eye sockets falling back to normal – or nearly normal – depth, the mouth still blackened around the perimeter of the lips, but somehow finding their original contour slowly instead of the bloated tribal orifice ... Skin on her body much drier, but tips of fingers ominously black and fingers rigid.

'At farm children quite happy with Stephen. Satu goes shopping. Stephen plays with Gabriel while Thomas industriously marches about. Read them story while Stephen fetches Satu. Pay Mrs Brideson. Find it difficult to "give" much to children, though, feel so drained by what has happened. When I say to Gabriel I want to tell him how Mummy is, he says no, that will make him too sad. Later though he whispers in my ear: "Tell me about the van." Seems to have his own or Roy's theory that Anna trying to burn out something painful in herself – and several times later says: "I think it's how I said." "She *will* survive, I think," he says to me, "because she's got much better very quickly." With Stephen's encouragement does a picture and some writing. Arrange Stephen to return to Bridget. My younger brother Martin to take them to sea again as yesterday.

'Back at hospital Anna lying with eyes open – very much better – must be the skin drying. Sight of her hands appals me – feel monumentally tired, finding it hard now to reassure her. Shortage of nursing staff – Anna worried by nurses, wants to sit up and see out. Finally nurse Jane takes over and I sleep fitfully but gratefully for 1½ hours. About 10 p.m. Martin comes – children had good afternoon and now asleep. "Everyone needs Daddy," Gabriel had said to me at lunchtime, "so Stephen and Martin are here instead when you have to go to Anna because we need a Daddy." Went for a walk with Martin about 10.30-ish – met consultant in street.

'"Hello Mr Reed," he said before I had spoken. Asked him *re* burned hands, movement of, etc. Said question of what areas can be saved, what amount of grafting possible, etc., can only be determined after 8–10 days; that it is still question of keeping her alive.

'Afterwards went up to Anna. Had had Valium – sleeping. Went to bed myself.'

7

Saturday, 23 June 1973

'Slept from 11.30-ish to 5.25 with constant dreams, occasionally aware of nurses turning Anna and changing linen. This time were turning, changing and spraying her – she seemed to be talking deliriously with occasional clear words the nurses could understand, but above all doing what they asked of her. Wanted coffee.

'When I went through the screens to her, faint smile. Yet her first impulse was to appeal: "Get me out of here!"

'I asked if she knew where she was and she shrugged. But when I tried to explain reasons for staying here she began to cut me short, saying I shouldn't always try to convince her, that I wouldn't listen to her, etc. "Get me out of here," kept repeating, "then I can see things from another perspective." Has to speak with minimum lip-movement, so painful. I said that if one were dying of injuries it would be wrong to move out until one was a bit better. But even here she snapped: "But if you're dying because of the way people speak to you!" I said ambulance would move her tomorrow, of course she wanted to go today...

'I asked nurse if Anna had had Valium – said yes, twice in night. Got her coffee ready. She seemed to calm a little, though in pain with weight of body tipped onto left arm. Suddenly seemed to recollect seriousness of her condition. "*Ist's wahr ich habe geschwebt zwischen Tod und Leben?* [Is it true I was hovering between life and death?]" she asks.

'Nurse says she had spoken in night of her mother. "She

would know how to make me better," she had said – otherwise confused and delirious, wanting to get out.

'Explain again how serious the burns are, that I've consulted many doctors about the best time to move her, that she must trust me there . . . Asked also if she'd like her mother to come over and be with her. "Yes," she whispers.

'Asks for something to eat – chicken broth.'

6.25 a.m.

'"David – tell me what happened."

'Begin to tell her – but uncomfortable and put pillow behind her back. Besides, what should I say that will not upset her, either now or later? Nurses come to change her and give her injection, so I went down with Martin who had come up about 7 a.m. – went with him to hotel to telephone Anna's mother.

'"*Ach, Gott,*" she cried when I said *how* Anna had done it – though fact itself almost expected I sensed somehow. Had a bath afterwards. When I got back to hospital Jane there – Anna quite lucid and aware for first time what had happened, extent of burns, etc., and how serious – though she says she doesn't remember how it happened. Jane suggests she read to her – so I go to car to get book and have breakfast – Anna having eaten poached egg, etc., for hers – sitting up on pillows with chest exposed and abdomen when I got back – asks for Illich essays to be read to her! Discusses educational practice and question of whether it is right to spank. Utterly extraordinary to listen to – absolute courage in her present state.

'"Mr Shifting Interest," she calls me as pain of antibiotic injections make her wince and cry out. Meanwhile consultant sees her, seems very pleased, also administrative sister. Then Anna wanted to be moved. Asked how: said more upright so that she could see me when I was talking to sister!

'Seems more and more aware of burn damage, talks of grafting, whether would be done under anaesthetic, etc. Sips tea, then as she is no longer comfortable I help Jane to change drawsheet and lay her down to sleep.

145

'She had even eaten a little lunch – mince, mashed potato and then jelly. Frightened, lips chattering, do not like to leave her – staff nurse going to sit with her.

'In the corridor downstairs I meet the doctor who had been on casualty duty the day Anna arrived. He sounds genuinely if stiffly pleased when I tell him that Anna is sitting, is eating, and so on. "But she is not out of the woods yet," he warns. "The grafting process itself brings further dangers – tissue rejection for one. It is a long, long process – and your wife has very little skin that can be spared for it."

'Only get back from lunch with Jane at three – seems that Anna had been very uncomfortable – had wrenched her name-band off – fingers bleeding from that. Staff nurse grateful to see me – says she had given Valium and morphine, but evidently not very effective – Anna agitated, a little feverish, mouth chattering, complaining of pain in the arm; tells me of name-band problem – had obviously got very upset at her second name being used as surname on the tag – thought it signified that we were divorced; and though she knew this was the case, did not wish to be reminded by tag! I tell her I had specifically asked yesterday that it be corrected and that she had herself said she didn't mind the name.

'"It isn't true what David says," had been her words when I'd said how she hated it. Seems tremendously relieved that I am with her now – "Well, you see, you weren't there!" she explains her outburst.

'Roy comes around 4. Anna already had more morphine (15mg), but still talking and aware. Roy talks to her for ½-hour; then while nurses turn her we go downstairs. Disagree *re* danger of her present mental state – R.L. thinks reaction normal given what has happened – I try to explain that delirium and loss/fear aspect exactly the same as *before* suicide attempt.

'R.L. leaves then – Anna still awake, a lot of pain from feet. Way she talks bears out Roy's view however – simply afraid of being left alone without the people she trusts. But in background is her fear and concern about scandal etc. to my family – she needs constant reassurance and is never really convinced. Very anxious I not leave her at night. Went to sleep straight away at

11.30, woken at 4 a.m. by Anna calling for me. Nurse with her says apparently Anna had not slept properly all night despite 20mg of morphine, and Valium as well. "David's better than Valium," says nurse. Sit with her then till about 5.30-ish when she begins to talk excitedly in French: "*Je suis le roi de Bourgogne-Chablis. Éloignez-vous. Scandale à votre famille. Je vous haïsse.*" Waving arm a great deal – terrible to see that charred black wreck of a hand. I sense the rigidity and violence of rejection which must have led to the suicide attempt, coming through despite morphine and Valium.

'Obviously pain/shame etc. unbearable and worsening: "*Mon dieu, mon dieu, ich kann nicht mehr* [I can't go on] ..." Extraordinary really that she has been spared pain – or too much pain – for so long. Obviously now beginning to activate again.'

8

Sunday, 24 June 1973

I have arranged that Martin will take the children to stay with some friends of mine. I will travel with Anna in the ambulance to the Regional Burns Unit.

The ambulance men come up at 8 a.m., use poles and a canvas sheet to transfer her to their stretcher-trolley. Most of the nursing staff in the hospital come to say good-bye – and good luck.

Nurse Jane is going with us. She is very responsible, very efficient, and knows this. Everything goes wrong.

As we are about to leave, an argument develops over the route we should take. The main control insists we go the shortest way; Jane insists we travel the long route, avoiding much hilly country. Instead of four hours the journey now takes six. Eventually and fortunately I fall asleep; Anna has had heavy dose of morphine and is not conscious. Inevitably, out of radio contact, we break down. A puncture: and the minutes tick by before Anna's sedative wears off.

'And he'd been driving so well!' says Jane.

It seems hours while the driver and his boy-assistant walk to the nearest house to telephone. Their telephone is out of order. A passing motorist must be stopped and asked to dial 999 in the next town. We don't even know where we are.

By chance an ambulance passes us from the other direction and our driver hails it. He gets permission to cancel his call and we transfer Anna's stretcher-trolley to his vehicle.

It begins to rain as we drive through the town. I see church spires, flyovers, blocks of houses being demolished for a motor-way. Then, a little way out of town, we turn off a country lane and the ambulance driver reports to the hospital admission point. There seems only series of elongated huts, single-storied, like an army camp, and we drive straight on, following the signs marked 'Burns Unit'.

We turn left past tall trees; here the buildings have sloping rather than flat roofs, and are set well apart from one another. A capped metal chimney smokes above the operating theatre. We drive past that too until we come to the ward. There is no one waiting. It is several minutes before a male orderly appears. Anna is conscious now. It has been an endless passage. I dread to think what the continuous jogging and jolting, then the transfer to a second ambulance, must have done to her.

The male nurse has a neatly trimmed beard like Anna's brother Berthold; he wheels her through a series of three- and four-bed wards till we reach the end of the building, rather like the last hospital. There is a patient already lying in this last two-bed room. Despite Anna's critical condition after the journey it is two hours before a doctor arrives. In the meantime no morphine can be administered without his signature. After all the talk about this hospital my heart sinks.

The doctor is a youngish surgeon, perhaps my own age. Having seen Anna he asks me into the sister's office. He apolo-gizes for having been so long – it is a Sunday and he is the only duty doctor there. He takes down some more notes, but his cheerfulness seems genuine. He says it is unlikely they will start doing any skin-grafting operations until the depth of the burns is revealed, and Anna's condition improves.

The senior Registrar arrives. He spends only a short time

examining Anna before he comes in. I listen to what he tells me, but I cannot believe what he says. Later I enter it in my diary.

'The Registrar declares the chances of recovery small – so much damage, of such a different nature than fractures or other form of accident – affecting whole metabolism.

'Roy would say: Anna has surprised us all, and maybe she still will. But without being self-pitying it is I who must bear the blame – I who took her out of the mental hospital, I who knew from the beginning that she was probably too fragile to cope with this trial à Laing – or did I lose my nerve, my determination in letting myself fall asleep?

'I feel sandwiched. I feel utterly exposed to guilt, to shame, to helplessness, to the absolute despair of having to watch power-lessly while, as a result of something I can never change, Anna dies. "If I had to choose between concentrating on my children and my wife, it would be the children," the Registrar says – and from the end of the ward I hear Anna screaming deliriously.

'By evening other patient moved out and the end ward closed off.

'Probability, to be discussed with consultant tomorrow, that Anna's hands will be crippled if she lives. "People have survived with worse burns," the Registrar says – but feels it right to explain that chances are against. Only over initial shock, stage 1 – haven't even started tissue problems.

'The second time in five days that a senior surgeon warns me of the improbability of survival, the second time Anna's probable death confronts me like the last page of a book that I do not wish to finish, the second time that somehow, somehow I must summon again the courage to *make* Anna live . . . Life without her seems so utterly unthinkable – not because it is practically impossible, but because her spirit is so profoundly the measure of it, of life, for me – and for the children.

'I think of the day she emerged – that morning by the stream . . . so much love, so much goodness and wonder, so much intelligence and vitality that is hers, hers alone . . .

'Went to sleep 10.30-ish.'

9

They do not allow me to sleep in Anna's room, despite the now empty bed, but I am given a room at the far side of the hospital, about half a mile away.

Monday, 25 June 1973

'Woke shortly after 5 a.m. – came over to ward – Anna crying out, delirious, no nurse anywhere. Talked with her, gave her water. Obviously in great pain and agitation (*"ich kann nicht mehr, ich kann nicht mehr"*) – talking of my elder brother and his wife Sophie, of my father and mother. "I don't want anything to do with your family" – yet how she liked Sophie (nurse later said she had been talking of Philippines). Had had morphine before midnight and again at 4.30, but apparently no effect. Also Valium. Called for Roy, her mother (particularly when in pain). Waving her arms ("tatty bags" she called them last night, for they have now been put into plastic bags, and the skin covered in special cream). Spoke of insecurity – wanted to go to East Berlin, then spoke of Moscow-Peking. Little Red Book. Also partition between "your poetry and German poetry". Kept saying name of Christoph Rathgens – her friend in Munich? Partition = split? the sense of sides? Throughout psychosis she had spoken of wanting to go, or having to go to the "other side" – whether of river in the country or neighbour's wall . . .

'When I say she must want to live she says Yes, she *does* want to live – interspersed with "*ich kann nicht mehr* . . ." Tell her she must sleep, and she promises – falls off about 7 a.m., though whimpering constantly. Outside the white vaporous clouds reveal the dawn, and disperse, and the sun begins to show its hazy circle. Obviously it is going to be a hot, clear day. I look out over the lawns, closely mown, covered with daisies.

'Write to Roy. Other questions so impossible to think about. And the children? How difficult yesterday to face their need of me when I carry in my soul the cries and distress of Anna. And their tears when I stayed here and they went home.

'Is there hope, I wonder? At the beginning, in the other hospital, I had to face up to the prospect of Anna's death; her life has now been saved, only to renew the struggle. I must keep separate all my own anxieties and feelings of guilt: they will not help her, they will not help me at this moment. I have to go on encouraging her to live, that is all: and in the face of a degree of pain and suffering, I would have succumbed long ago, I know.'

10

I stay the night with the children at my friend's house, about forty-five minutes' drive away. But Anna's condition meanwhile worsens.

Tuesday, 26 June 1973

'Woke at 5 a.m. – Thomas awake at 7 a.m., Gabriel to school at 9 a.m. – headmistress very nice. Telephoned London, played with Thomas. Left at 11.20 for hospital. Mother-in-law there, said Anna had asked where I was and been told I was taking children to school, at which she was quite content – same last night apparently says the sister. However about ½-hour later opened eyes when I spoke – eyes glazed and far away. Very weak it seemed. Told her about Gabriel going to school, and the system of family-grouping there and she smiled understandingly. Gave her a little tea, sat her up with nurse to make it easier to swallow. "Thank you David," she murmured audibly. Little later talked a bit more. I told her how deeply, deeply I love her – at first she seemed consoled by it, but then she murmured "*nicht wahr* [not true]". I repeated and repeated it till at last I think she began to believe me. "Do you remember when we went to France together?" I asked – and Anna nodded, smiled. "How terribly in love I was with you . . ."

'Asked to leave while dressings changed – Anna given morphine, I went to see social worker. Went back – Anna asleep. Looking very bad. Ask nurse in blue about depth of burns, etc. Only 2 deaths in 4½ years she has witnessed, she says. "I must just be lucky," she says in West Country accent. Eventually feel quite faint with distress and leave, pass chapel, go in, ask chaplain to pray with me. Wept and wept. Canteen closed, meet chaplain (new vicar of parish) again afterwards and go to his house for tea – has 4 children. Find I can hardly eat, same with drink – sheer nerves. Return. Anna barely conscious – her mother there who had said I was fetching Gabriel from school. Spoke to Anna myself – eyes even more glazed. Sister says she has the feeling Anna more poorly than yesterday, should not plan beyond day to day. Ring house at 6.45 – but already Anna has murmured "*ich schaffe es nicht mehr, ich schaffe es nicht* [I won't make it any more, I won't make it]", rolling glazed eyes slowly, focussing on me, and closing them. Priest comes and we all pray; about 8 morphine begins to wear off, obviously, for gradually Anna starts taking more drinks. "*Gott hat mir Flügel gegeben. Gott hat uns Flügel gegeben* [God gave me wings, God gave us wings]", she says. Begins to sing: Tuscany, Tuscany . . . Then Amory, Amory, Amory. Amory of London? Yes. (Later says, talking as if to Amory, that wants Amory, her friend, to be responsible for children.)

'"*Fackelbearer* [torchbearer]" she also chants, and bits of Lieder. Seems like the end. I talk to her of God, and all I say she then sings. "God will give us strength . . ."

'"So many people died . . .," she chants.

'I say we all have to die, God will decide when.

'And lo, out of this seemingly dying state she emerges, quite lucidly and loudly; eyes still glazed, but less so – accepts great quantity of juice and even Complan and milk when I suggest it. Amory is blessed she had kept chanting, while I repeatedly said that she too was blessed. "Mary Barnes – will she forgive me?" she asks – and I read her Mary's card. "Mary understood – she touched me – she understood my problems. I couldn't face it. I couldn't face it" – but will not say what it was. Somehow – even after phone call from her brother in which I had to explain the

152

situation – hope rising again: to a crescendo. Will God allow her to live? What seemed cruel – to prolong such suffering – only an hour ago, now seems so different, so much strength and courage there – still surprising us as Roy would say – though even if she survives next week the struggle is by no means over – will be continuing battle against infection and death: yet with at least, despite the pain, the actual *possibility* of life!'

11

Wednesday, 27 June 1973

'Woke at 5 a.m. – came over to ward. Anna sleeping. When she wakes her eyes are distant, very very weak, as though in a far, far-off place. Mutter comes over 7-ish, but does not return to her hotel for breakfast as Anna remains awake. Simon, the vicar/chaplain, calls. I tell Anna – and she asks him to stay, which he does. We all say Amen, Mutter weeping, and I could not stop my own tears. Then Anna spoke a prayer herself in German: "*Vergib' mir meine Sünden. Herr Gott, Herr Gott, vergib' mir meine Sünden, rache es nicht an meinen Kindern!* [Forgive my sins. Dear God, dear God, forgive my sins, do not make my children suffer for them!]." Simon must have caught the gist, for he said another prayer: "O Lord, forgive our sins, let thy light and thy strength come upon us . . ."

'After he had gone, Anna said with a deep sigh: "*Jetzt kann ich sterben* [now I can die]" – and if all the agony since last Wednesday were to come again, it would still have been worth it for that moment of confrontation. Whatever happens now will not, in a sense, matter; whether God gives her the strength to survive or the strength to die, this moment will have been crucial.

'Spoke to Consultant – Anna had been awake and I'd told her who it was when he came in. Seems pleased with general condition, despite my own feeling about weakness in that respect: said it was important not to tire her – going to go on giving morphine to help conserve her strength for the real battle, the toxin battle, which begins next week, when dead skin gradually poisons whole bloodstream. Said that was when Anna would most need me, to see the children as much as possible now.

'Go to see the children then, as Anna asleep. Thomas obviously delighted to see me. Had lunch, saw Satu off on train. Pouring with rain. Collect Gabriel from school. Face beaming, Dominic's too, as we came up road, few minutes late. "We *looked* for you up there!" Dominic says, pointing to where Mums congregating.

'At home Gabriel and Dominic play contentedly with knights, and I read Thomas a story. Teatime with ice-cream; bed quite early, after bath which Patrick manages himself – read Gabriel and Dominic *Tintin*: children stay awake for a while, but Thomas seeming quite content.

'Left 9 p.m. for the hospital. Anna asleep at first, but soon wakes. I feel so desperately tired. Morphine wears off late evening. Anna obviously anxious – talks of Noah and Eigenheim, pursuing own ends at expense of others, or roughly so, chanting the words – got very voluble at one stage, talking to Noah, telling him to go away – is Noah an evil figure in her ideas? Settles at 10.30 – talk with her mother till midnight about getting a girl to help with the children. Encouraging her to see Anna as a person, not her bodily condition, and her life as her own, with its own time-span, not simply the one we would neatly wish it to have – whether to save her suffering or our own.'

12

Thursday, 28 June 1973

'Woken in visitor's ward by telephone at 6 a.m. – nurse says Anna had a reasonably peaceful night, no change in her condition, but awake if I'd like to be with her.

'Went over straight away – eyes astonishingly clear when she opens them, but skin area of lips and all round perimeter beginning to break up in crusts like canyons – nose also looking more charred, on forehead can now see tiny veins beneath surface as once on her legs – confirms horribly Consultant's impression regarding face.

154

'Seems happy that I'm there, though finding it difficult to speak, murmuring more and more. Had had morphine injection at 5 a.m., but no sign of real sleep. Seems still in pain. Calls "Mutti!" frequently. Morphine given again, but not very effective – fitful and anxious all morning. My father rings, coming tomorrow. Write last piece for my arts page in waiting-room while Anna's sheets supposed to be changed. "Sarah [the manager of the shop] *hat gewonnen* [Sarah's won]," she had murmured earlier. "*Wann willst Du den Contract?* [When will you make the contract?]" Assure her no question of giving up the shop to Sarah. On the contrary Sarah wishes to leave it. It is for our children, hers and mine ...

'Now, with eyes open, I see such spirit left; such great great courage after all that has happened, and I cry with shame and distress that the path we are striving to find is now so irrevocably removed. Had it been barbiturates or even slashing her wrists again, she might have quickly been saved: whereas now the odds are so heavy against us: and the children so young ...

'Only went to sleep around 1 p.m., nurses about to do her dressing. Finish last newspaper piece, rewrite second one, do layout instructions, put in envelope, and post. Back at Patrick and Megan's at ten past three, walk up to collect Gabriel and Dominic. Feeling so tired. Warm and sunny afternoon, children appear with their teacher at 3.30, line up and disperse. Gabriel so young and princely – take off their coats. Watch as Gabriel runs down the road after Dominic: the grace and wonder of his body as he moves, hair flying, leaping into life always. When I see Megan wheeling Thomas and Susan together can only cry.

'Play with them at home – in garden with football, on bikes, with Matchbox cars etc.: slowly unwind, give them the love and patience that Anna would want me to – would give herself. Think how much Anna gives me, even in this torment. "My mother loves you," she said this morning; "but she is awkward and can't show it easily" – how characteristic of Anna to think of others, even of me, when she herself is in such pain. It was when I was weeping that she said it. And like our whole life, the courage she gives me by her very being *is* something I can return, both to her and to others.

'Though not drinking very much at the moment she seems much stronger than yesterday.

'Talk to Peter on phone about help, and James Preston in London. Put children to bed – Thomas goes to sleep all right, but very fitful sleep, almost like Anna, waking constantly. Worries me. Rang Mutter at hospital – she sounded anxious – Landis there and Anna's temperature rising sharply (8 p.m.) – obviously first toxin/poison testing her strength. I said I'd come over later. Roy sounding very upset, as though crying.

'Arrived hospital 11.30 p.m. – Anna rousable when I spoke but taking only brief note. Breathing seems harder. Bandage under chin where they are trying to soften hardened skin. Area round lips still broken and strange: but this clearness of her eyes and the strength of her breathing (pulse 150) don't suggest that she is too weak to withstand it. Somehow I feel only life is there, by no means death: as though the courage she herself has given me, and the love of our children had increased my own hope and spirit. Feel only strength. Send mother home, sit with Anna till 1.30, then fall asleep in armchair – wake at 2.30 and go over to visitors' ward. Apparently Roy had told her not even to think of dying – was adamant she should live! Mutter in a bit of a state about him.

'Anna had chanted and sung, and talked a bit – rather incoherently. I was woken at 6.30 a.m. – nurse said she'd called for me. Breathing definitely laboured, otherwise temperature right down, and really quite resolute in face. Talks about Inge, Inge, Axel-Springer, money – articulation becoming more difficult to understand.

13

I keep no record for Friday: it's the day my father comes up with my mother from London, having insisted on the telephone that they cannot stay any longer 'on the end of a telephone' through all this without seeing me.

I'm with Anna all day. In the evening I put all the children to bed as Patrick and Megan are going out. My mother and father arrive: but then give presents to the children, who are still awake and who subsequently become too excited to go back to bed or sleep. When Patrick and Megan return, early, the children are still awake. Then my father begins his inevitable soliloquy about trade unions. It's all so damned polite – and Anna isn't even mentioned.

I feel like breaking something – insist I must sleep and usher them away. They are to take the children to the zoo on Sunday.

14

Saturday, 30 June 1973

'Woke about 7, Gabriel and Thomas still asleep. Still raging over last night's fiasco. In end I simply run back to hospital – where Anna's mother with her. Says she is delirious. Sat with Anna. Obviously very afraid, talking of conspiracies, wants me to take her out, says I don't know what she knows. Does not say who "they" are. Irritated at my disinclination – but by talking with her, sitting with her, she soon begins to emerge: eyes quite clear now, and able to focus in different directions. Again seems to have forgotten why or how she is here – cannot believe about burns – try to get her to look at her hands. Slowly it sinks back. But once again I feel her braveness rising – braveness of spirit, innate spirit – and spirit as a sort of fire itself, that burns, and cannot be extinguished. I ask her if she knows why she did it – she had seemed to recollect more, once the existence of the burns was established – and she nods.

'"Can you tell me?" I ask.

'It is then that the answer, the reason, emerges for the first time in ten days as far as I know.

'"I was Hitler."

'"Hitler?" It seems incredible. But apart from the burning of his corpse in petrol . . .?

'"But what possible connection could you see between yourself and Hitler?"

'She closes her eyes. I wait.

'"I'd done so much bad . . ."'

'Can it really be so? She starts to show pain, says on the soles of her feet. Ask if she wants to be turned – get nurse to help me – screams as nurse put her hands under her back and tilts her towards me to shift her. Nurse asks if she wants anything for the pain – she says no, it's all right if she can talk to someone . . . Extraordinary, her childlike goodness and courage.

'Incident with ambulance men – breeze in like KGB men just as Anna talking of her fears of abduction and conspiracy. Call her "my love" and "dear" – so she calls one of them back as he reaches the door – addresses him in French: "*Monsieur, vous devez comprendre – comment dit-on – que quand vous m'adressez des mots comme ça, c'est très gentil, mais . . .*"' And the men retreat in shame and confusion – that is when I *know* they are not doctors, despite the white coats!

'She says: "You know what I'd like . . . some fruit." Nurse offers oranges – but she asks for raspberries. I offer strawberries. "But what month is it?"

'"End of June – there are plenty in the shops. Would you like me to get you some?"

'Now, after her mother's pessimistic head-shaking this morning, the situation has yet again been reversed. Anna wanting strawberries! And taking soup quite happily – even blowing her nose successfully, which had been blocked. Unbelievable.

'"Yes, you can go, if the nurse only promises not to move me!" she says – and we all laugh.

'Takes a little to persuade her that I ought to be with the children. Says naturally she would like to see them, if only for a moment. Also her brother. Tell her he has rung, is in Germany. She says she wants him to come.

'"I might not see him again," she says.

'So awake and *alive*, she gets quite fed up with me I think. Senses the very least "stock" nature in my responses. "David, I love you very much," she will say, "but when you are cynical

158

I can't bear it . . ." "Are you going now?" – as though driving me away.

'Home at 2 p.m. Go to fête at 3 with children – donkeys, go-karts, balloons – and the Red Devils Parachute Brigade – seven men in all, diving out with red flares; then parachutes opening only perhaps 1,000 feet above ground.

'Return home – try to get children to help clean car, hoping thus to exorcise awkward association?

'Go over to hospital late, after children asleep, since Anna's mother seems anxious on phone: instead find Anna breathing heavily but still very strongly – no cause for alarm. Go to bed visitors' ward 11 p.m., wake at 7 a.m.'

15

Sunday, 1 July 1973

'Woke 7 a.m. – could not move till 7.30, as though paralysed by continual loss of sleep, despite knowing cannot go back to sleep again. Anna asleep – snoring loudly, face thin – body too, as though she has lost a lot of weight. Wakes only at 9.15 – and what a smile! Like the return of the prodigal child!

'"Good morning," she murmurs – eyes strong and clear again – only when she half-closes them and slips back into slumber do they seem distant and faded. "I feel so happy," she says after greeting the cleaning woman too with a wonderful smile.

'"Was I very ill last night?" she asks. I tell her it's the eleventh night now. "It feels longer," she murmurs. Wants to dictate something, but too weak. "Family . . ." Then: ". . . friends who don't mind if Gabriel is Scottish and don't mind playing with him. Gabriel . . ."

'Sleeps.

'Asks about Berthold, her brother. I say he should be there any minute – and lo and behold, he walks past window – asks for a moment to compose himself before going in. Leave him with Anna for a while.

'After lunch – at which Anna has soup, a peach, and asks for ice-cream! – Roy arrives suddenly with Patty. He asks to be left alone with Anna. "I see you kept your side of the bargain," he begins – Anna a little delirious still and constant amnesia – R.L. says: "You burned yourself. You're in a medical hospital. You nearly gave up on us. The staff here seemed to feel that you didn't stand much of a chance."

'Afterwards he asks me to see doctors about move to London – suggests two ambulances to obviate disaster similar to last time. Gets on my nerves, and I tell him bluntly I'm not risking Anna's life in her present critical condition just to make it half an hour easier for him to visit her – I feel bad saying it, but once again I resent his assumptions.

'Berthold worried about sterilization and hygiene – clearly resents Patty.

'Then Anna has morphine. My father and mother arrive – children very pleased to see me (Thomas fast asleep in the car to begin with), and we sit on the lawn outside the wards. Ask my father if he would like to see Anna. Says yes rather determinedly.

'"Poor, poor girl," he murmurs when we go in – Anna at first asleep, face somehow blacker than usual. "On her best days, one of the most beautiful faces I've ever seen," he says.

Gabriel at first anxious, unwilling to go in van. My father offers to take him – but then he says no, wants to go with Daddy, Driving away I say to Gabriel that Anna has been talking about him.

'"That's what you say every day!" Gabriel complains – and I am acutely aware that I am doing no differently from my own father – only today it happens to be true. Remarkable how he sees through any conscious attempt to comfort him. He spoke quite openly in front of my father about Anna burning herself. "She wanted to burn it out . . ." he explains with emphasis and concentration.

'Stay the night at Patrick's – good sleep.'

16

Monday, 2 July 1973

'Take Gabriel to school; Thomas cries when I leave (10 a.m.) but somehow I feel he will cope, and the tears are good tears. Anna smiles brightly when I come – her mother says she can't make sense of what Anna says. Meanwhile Anna seems mainly frightened – CIA she mentions once. Wants me to take her out at all costs – again not aware why she is there really. Begins to doze – eyes very clear though, remarkably so. When doctors come in they both remark on how well she looks. I say: "She'll stop believing you if you say it too often – everyone seems to be saying it this morning."

'"What lovely eyes she has," one nurse had said to another as they cleaned her mouth.

'I felt very drowsy. Sister does not suggest any lunch for Anna, so I ask kitchen staff for an egg at 1 p.m. She takes it very well, though obviously very tired.

'Berthold stays, and I check local estate agents for a flat – no luck. Collect Gabriel – aura of peace at home, though Gabriel is fed up with Dominic and plays separately. Obviously getting tired at school now as novelty wears off. Difficult to get them to go to sleep.

'Stay up reading novel – utter rubbish. Children wake at 1 a.m. – Gabriel complaining of sore throat. Prepare Disprin, but Gabriel asleep when I take it up to him. A bad omen?'

17

Tuesday, 3 July 1973

'Take children to school in van. Anna asking for me and "aggressive" according to her mother. Nurse very angry, says Anna's mother was there till 2.30 a.m. and kept Anna awake –

shouldn't be allowed! Apparently someone has spoken to her, though.

'Anna pleased to see me. Mutter gives me address of Mrs Trent – Anna picks up name instantly. "Now you go to the Trent woman," she says – chance of a house just outside hospital gates. Anna's face extraordinary well, despite the way the skin on her chin is forming an outer crust now that no longer moves in time with the inner one. Eyes very clear, able to focus anywhere, alert and bossy.

'I go. Success – wonderful flat on top of Georgian house – don't like to get too excited though. Return – burns being dressed – went to canteen for coffee and saw social worker. When returned Anna still fantastically alert, but seething over pain of dressings removal. Some blood on her face – arguing with sister (fortunately very personable and forbearing and young) – calls her Annie. Quite unbelievable to see Anna so *well*: temperature only little above normal, pulse 130s. Some stitching on left shoulder – why? Wish I could take upon myself some of the sheer *pain*. Then Anna asks sister for *lunch*! Meat!

'Gets fish, potato and veg! And eats lot of it – chewing like a healthy woman! Can only shake my head. Wants cigarette too – to which sister accords – doesn't work out, though, as Anna unable to suck.

'Gets a bit tired of me and sends me away as the pain intensifies and eventually I have to get nurse to give injections. Seems such a very natural response, really.

'Take children to the sea. Tide way out – children running over sand, picnic – but how sad to be living "alone" with children – how I miss Anna's presence, her *spirit*!

'Tell story of Little Bright Thing and the Crab on way home – seems successful.'

18

Wednesday, 4 July 1973

'Berthold leaves – Anna's mother had been there till midnight and again from 5 a.m. – pointless as far as I can see. Nurse says Anna's mother has had a premonition. Doing Anna no good, though. Fever again at midday.

'In afternoon take children to the sea again, this time to swimming pool first. Very beautiful warm evening – pale red dusk, the almost deserted sand ... Didn't get back till 8.45. Gabriel awake with a sore throat. Patrick in kitchen says doesn't believe in psychology because it is "dangerous" – instances Anna's case when I ask him to elucidate.

'Is he afraid? Identifying his own marriage ...?

19

Thursday, 5 July 1973

'Take children to school – growing dissension between Gabriel and Dominic. At the hospital Anna's temperature is shooting up again – from 37° to 39.6° in a couple of hours. Nurse says there is nothing one can do – with such large burns the skin cannot control in normal way. Sleeps. Go and buy present for Patrick and Megan. Return to their house. Peter and new children's help already there. Gloria, she is called, blonde-haired, rotund, wide fat face with an apple on bosom of her T-shirt. Makes little effort unless asked. Fear the worst.

'Leave after collecting Gabriel from school – the house is a godsend.'

But Gloria turns out to be wonderful with the children. She thinks constantly of their needs, and is aware of their individual natures. With her, in the big Georgian mansion, on the common, in the walled gardens behind the house and with the hamster on the lawn – she is a presence they come to trust implicitly. Mrs Trent is in her seventies, a dear, tiny woman, a sort of classic Edwardian lady, totally self-reliant, whether driving, cooking, gardening, or reading detailed archaeological reports on nearby digs. She has that boundless blue-eyed curiosity – a sort of mix of humility and intelligence, the rare ability to go on celebrating youth in old age . . .

It cannot all be coincidence, it must be part of a pattern. On Friday Anna undergoes her first major operation, at least a week before expected. She comes out of the anaesthesia in the early afternoon as though she has just returned from a bracing, invigorating holiday. I am told she will be drowsy, possibly in pain: instead she is as bright as a button.

Scaffolding bars now make a sort of four-poster canopy-frame over the bed; and an assortment of pulleys and wide, solid circular weights support her tightly bandaged legs in the air like a piece of Heath Robinsonia. They have 'cleaned' the entire surface of her legs and thighs to form a base for skin-grafting. Everyone is astonished by her recovery.

Dear James,

Thank you and Miranda for writing to me. If it's hard for me even to telephone please don't imagine that I've sunk into total withdrawal – it's simply that the nature of Anna's injuries, the fact that I must live with the possibility, even probability, of her death for the next three months or more makes it impossible for me to lift either pen or receiver. In the end it is only I who can come to terms with the reality, it cannot be shared, nor fate tempted by over-confidence. Anna is well – unbelievably well considering that she had a three-hour operation only this morning: but it is tomorrow and the following day that will be critical – and the same process will repeat itself with each subsequent operation . . .

Sometimes I wonder whether I can take so much grief and empathy: how I can possibly keep myself whole and alive for the children, for instance, when so much is at stake; yet curiously, it is from Anna herself I draw my real courage. Her spirit, her unique spirit has flowered these past few weeks in a way which seems to grip the entire hospital – from cleaners to nursing staff, from doctors to fellow patients. The miracle of her recovery to date is on everyone's lips – and Anna's sheer bravery in the face of seemingly fatal burns. Yesterday she asked if I could obtain some marijuana for her; and when I asked why, she said because today she would be dead! She talks in three languages, tried to marry off one of the nurses to Peter, and when told one evening the young male nurse would be looking after her during the night, exclaimed: 'Oh good! I rather like him!'

Nothing I can write on this card can convey the miraculous nature of these days: except perhaps if I say that *whatever* happens – whether Anna is spared or must die – the courage she shows now is something no one here will ever, ever forget.

Love,
David

20

Saturday, 7 July 1973

'Woke at 5 a.m., then 7 a.m. – fitful sleep, nervous dreams – children waking and whimpering between 11 p.m. and 1 a.m. Cannot help wondering if it's telepathic. Try not to.

'Children woke – played in their room for an hour till 8 a.m.; I lay in a sort of stupor till 9 while Gloria looked after them. Read *The Waste Land* which happened to be beside my bed – somehow (after what I have been through?) its originality has become commonplace and its rhymes too light.

'For almost the first time I began to wonder whether I can cope.

'Went over to hospital at 9.30 – Anna wide awake, being fed milk. Nurse gives me the bottle. Cold. Anna asks for warm milk – smiles when I say Miss Bossy Boots. "Bright as a button she's been this morning," says nurse. Seems to have had good rest last night. We talk a little. Then Anna announces she would like "*richtige Analyse* [proper analysis]" – as opposed to "irrational" forms she is currently receiving – Landis and the rest.

'Then doctor comes to take blood. After he has gone, I ask her what she means. Says that current analysis not bad, but can only go "so far". I ask if she feels it put too much pressure on her – says yes. But the alternative? She could have stayed at the mental hospital and had ECT.

'"You wouldn't have wanted that, would you?" I ask.

'"No. But then I wouldn't have wanted this," she remarks.

'I feel stunned – and relieved – when she says she can't take any more talking, would like me to go. Ask if she wants me to come back in afternoon or evening – evening she says.

'"And do you want your mother to come?"

'"No. But you can give her a letter ... Tell her I'm getting better."

'For the first time I feel she really *knows* what is up. She had said, "But it is you who are burned," and such like, too, I know – but that last remark puts it beyond doubt. "I wouldn't have wanted this."

'"Is my face so terrible?"

'How do I answer that? I say, to someone who doesn't know you it might appear a little frightening – and she answers my face too could be that!!

'"I don't want to become a drug addict," she says (concerning morphine).

'Seems very surprised when they tell her has pins through her legs.

'Physically she appears to be in an extraordinary condition considering that the operation was only yesterday. Blood pressure steady, T P R and respiration fine, drinking gallons, ice-cream for breakfast ...

'I came away in a daze – knowing I was already deeply depressed this morning. It is the recurring sense of guilt, of having exposed Anna unnecessarily to an injury which cannot be undone, which if it does not take her life will cripple her for the rest of it ...'

'Children playing with Mutter in "secret" garden. Lunch. In the afternoon the Horse Show – surprising how Thomas runs off on his own there, seemingly unperturbed and not in the least frightened of losing me: whereas at home he still cries if I even go upstairs without him. Buy flowers and take them to Anna at about a quarter to five – temperature rather high (39°) and seems to want me to stay with her, so Mutter takes the children home. Anna eats chicken and ice-cream; but drip-feed runs dry and student nurse cannot get it going again. Leave about 8.45 and tell children a story, have supper, and return. Mutter at window indicates that Anna is going to sleep – though I distinctly hear her singing. Meet Mutter at end of corridor – says Anna asleep almost for over an hour; nurse giving her an injection. Calm her down. Explains she has seen R. D. Laing in corner, who had wanted her to go on a "trip" with him. "I like him very much, he's very charming; but I didn't want to go. He said it would only mean leaving David for a few weeks or months, but I told him I didn't want to. I mean, he's very nice, he had it all arranged – a rocket ready to take us up . . ."

'Takes hours to settle her – wants me to sleep in her bed to keep her warm! New drip still only barely running, complaining of much pain – finally leave at midnight.

'When I offer to read letter from Patty which I find in bedside cabinet, Anna waves it away.

'"Another time. Patty is so intense . . ."'

21

Sunday, 8 July 1973

'Woke latish – children came in. Got up after 9 a.m. Went over to Anna at eleven – had just woken after sleeping since 8 a.m. Night very restless and no sleep apparently, despite Mogadon. Mother left then.

'"*Wenn meine Mutter nicht da ist, geht's mir blendend* [when my mother's not there I feel perfect]," she whispers to me. Still very frightened – wants me to stay overnight. Says night nurse never there to keep her company. Then asks for grapefruit!

'Under impression she has killed Gabriel. Anxious to leave the place.

'Located tin of grapefuit in kitchens. Fetch and feed her with some – then leave while dressings being changed. Children playing on common with Mutter – post letters and buy a few things.

'Vicar with children. Says he saw Anna yesterday afternoon

and had a ten-minute talk with her – surprised at her lucidity. She had said something very significant before he left which I might understand. She has asked where I was – and being told I was now the vicar's neighbour and thus living very close at hand in a flat which his wife had helped to get, Anna had gone quiet and then suddenly said: "If you try to help, you will get hurt."'

'Go over to ward after lunch. Gunhilda comes at about 3. Goes in and Anna immediately recognizes her; talks about Laing – says shouldn't have gone on the trip, that she was too young, her children were too small . . .

'Surprised Gunhilda by insisting that she should also have a cup of Ribena and some of the apple I was giving her. Then seemed to fall asleep, and we went out, talking in waiting-room.

'SEN passes saying Anna asking to see me – no, demanding! Go down – a lot of blood under sheet from a haemorrhage. Doctor called immediately – loses quite substantial amount. Becomes very sleepy, dozes off, and I go home to put children to bed and have supper. Thomas asleep already. Gloria says Gabriel sleepwalking. Talk about them. Father phones.

'Return to ward. Anna asleep for further hour. Then mistakes me for someone else – smiles with delight when she realizes. Says she thought I was going away from her, leaving her with short hair . . . Feels that doctor has made incision with a knife. Talks a bit about the mental hospital and the country – "wonderful few days". Then she had left farmhouse because she "didn't want to share it with others" – and when I ask what and whom she means, she says the quality of it with Mary Barnes et al.

'I feel so tired. Stay with Anna till 11 p.m. when she begins to sleep again. Can hardly keep my eyes open to write this . . .'

Perhaps most difficult of all – more difficult even than the sight, the reality of her condition, three-quarters of her body ravaged by burns – are Anna's moments of insight into what happened, her revelations. I feel crucified by them.

Monday, 9 July 1973

'Woken at 6 a.m. by Gabriel – says his throat is sore – falls asleep in my bed; then Thomas comes over and has no intention of sleeping. Had breakfast and then came over about 9 a.m. Anna awake – cleaner (the one with the German husband) telling her I was coming. Looks fairly well – lips parched and cracked – thirsty. Said she had not slept – not in the least hysterical. Show her pictures of children – does not immediately recognize Gabriel. Again spoke of time when the healing will be over. Wants "good" analyst – this said *à propos* her fears of a Chinese invasion. Says that was her belief in the country – that she had burned herself as she didn't have the courage to kill the children. But even if the Chinese *were* to come why kill the children? I ask.

'" To save them from the six hours of torture," she says.

'I ask if fear of Chinese could have anything to do with childhood fear of Russians? Says yes.

'"What would be the matter with continuing analysis with Roy?" I ask.

'"When he comes back?"

'She is surprised when I tell her Landis hasn't gone away.

'"I'm very angry with him," she explains.

'"Why?"

'"Because he ought to have known."

'"Known?"

'"He should have seen that some people have tendencies . . ."

'"But would you have wanted ECT at the mental hospital?"

'"Well, if I'd had it at the beginning. I don't think it did any good to go through all that –"

'My heart sinks as my worst fears are confirmed. Intuition had told me right at the beginning Anna could ill cope with it all, however theoretically attractive Laing's ideas . . .

'"Was Berthold affected by the burns?" she asks – as though he might have been burned as well.

'"Where was I the first two days? What did they give me?"

'Then the Registrar comes in. Asks Anna how she is.

'"Not so bad," Anna answers.

'"Not so grand," he repeats mistakenly. Significant misinterpretation, as it appears. Asks to speak to me. Asks whether I am willing to give skin if no other available. Rings mortician – none. Smiles at mortician's reply that there are "two good ones in fridge", but no permission to use them. (Only if a post-mortem is required is one allowed to touch a body.)

'Then, finally, agrees to fill me in a little on Anna's chances.

'"I can see you've been stimulated by your wife's progress," he begins, "and you probably think that I was wrong to paint such a black picture in the beginning. Certainly her response up to now is remarkable. But," and he turns back to me, "I still hold to what I said. She's not out of the woods at all. She's still a very sick woman. She's still getting fevers. There's the catheter, and she could get septicaemia.

'"I'm not saying she couldn't survive – some people have. But I've seen cases like this so often. They survive the first operation, the second – and then complications set in. I've seen it before. And if she were to survive – I mean she'll never be able to look after the children again . . ."

'I explain how in fact she had not been able to do that fully even before the present circumstances – that I am not building any false hopes; but that Anna is alive and lucid, and that if these are her last weeks, then I wish to spend them with her. And if she is crippled – well, that is not something I fear; she has never been an outgoing person. He seems to find this difficult to understand. Says he couldn't take his family in too large doses without seeing people, having challenges – only reads for relaxation, entertainment, relief now. I say yes, medical training is in many ways damaging to the personality, so much study. He nods, says you have to be schizophrenic to be a good doctor! We talk on.

'But, inside, his first pronouncement has left me floored again – the sheer hopelessness of all this struggle, the hopelessness of hope. I refuse to believe Anna will die because she is so full of spirit at the moment; but logically I know that could change very suddenly.

'"You must be prepared for the worst, no good buoying up your hopes," he says. No; but this is present reality, with Anna alive, lucid, awake – that is the world I am living in at present, and the other one – the cost of the flat, the girl, and so on – is so utterly irrelevant at this moment.

'See Anna.

'"Well," she asks, "what did you talk about?"

'I say: "Being."

'"Always so vague!" Anna clips – though she cannot know what it costs me to face her after this kind of prognosis.

'Go home when they start to change dressings. Morphine and sleep p.m.'

It is agreed that the operation will take place the next day. They will take the top layer of skin from my thighs – from pelvis to knees. In the evening I take a bath and shave my legs with a razor they have given me. And if it were to go wrong? Somehow, for the very first time in my life – except perhaps those nights at home while Anna was still psychotic – *I do not care if I am to die.*

9.7.73

Dear Roy,

Gunhilda came down yesterday and will have filled you in by now. Like everyone who comes into contact with Anna at the moment Gunhilda seemed overwhelmed by Anna's radiance, seemingly unperturbed either by her injuries or the major operation she went through on Friday. It is truly something of a miracle; and yet one cannot pretend that fate is now on her side. The Senior Registrar continues to paint a black picture – not, I think, because they have in any way given up, but because experience teaches them to be sceptical until a patient actually stands up and walks out of the hospital. Nor do I quarrel with this attitude – his job is to do everything medically possible to save Anna's life; it is mine to hope that she will live.

Much more distressing than the doctor's refusal to show optimism, however, is Anna's own attitude towards what has happened. Pointless to conceal that she feels angry towards you, feels you failed to recognize the danger of her suicidal tendencies, that the weeks of psychosis were unnecessary and could have been halted at the beginning ... I retell this not to hurt you, Roy, but because it hurts *me* so much. Your commitment to recovery from 'schizophrenia' by confrontation goes beyond Anna and is undamaged by failure in a particular case; whereas for me the position is quite other. I only have one Anna; and while believing profoundly in my obligation to help her achieve a better life – whether with me or even at the cost of having to leave me – every intuitive sense inside me cautioned against exposing her to the sort of trauma which 'going down' must inevitably be. In other words it was I who metaphorically put the match into her hand, all the time piously believing that I was acting in her own interest. If she lives I can try to show her that it was not in vain: that some trial like this was perhaps the only alternative to a life of recurrent breakdown and sense of failure. But if she dies?

Gunhilda asked about visiting etc., and I found it hard to give a straightforward answer. Anna's will to live is simply not in question at the moment, she is very strong. The nursing staff resent too many visitors because they feel it is exhausting Anna when she needs all the rest and calm she can get under such painful circumstances. On the other hand it is important, in terms of her continual fears and phantasies of plots, conspiracies, bugging, scandal, invasion, murder, etc., that recognizable faces from outside should appear – they are by far the best way of dispelling such states of anxiety.

I shall stop here, though there is so much more to say. I love Anna and only seem able to cope at that level: any wider issues – guilt, responsibility, death – leave me shattered.

Love, David

23

Tuesday, 10 July 1973

'Wake at 5 a.m.; get up at 6.30; over at ward at 6.50 – nobody about, so peaceful. Wondering whether I should have made a last will! Get undressed, put on white bed-gown, take off rings etc., take pre-med pills. Three men talking in and beside next bed, cannot get to sleep at all – ask sister for my Conrad; read a few pages about how he wrote *Nostromo* (he thought he had written himself out already), started the story – and the next I knew poles were being slid on both sides of me, I was lifted onto a trolley-bed and wheeled outside – sister and the theatre boy pushing me up ramp. Along corridor – doors on each side, fluorescent lights. Then a woman in green tie-down theatre cap asking me my name – Is your name David Branwen Reed? Yes. Made me flex and ease my fingers and wrist, rubbed back of my hand. I could see the anaesthetist I had met the night before, and in went the needle – pushing into the back of my hand. Do you feel yourself falling asleep? the woman asked – and I turned my head over to the other side, to Sister, to tell her something – that I loved Anna?

'Woke later – thigh stinging – seemed to be about 11.30 a.m. – 2½ hours after going in. Nurse came in with syringe, I wanted to get out of bed, the pain in the thighs was so cruel I felt only by distracting myself, by putting weight on my feet, could I bear it. Then for a moment it seemed to get better and I sent her away – too soon, too optimistic, alas, for not long later I was calling for her, she told me to roll over . . .

'Woke in the afternoon – talked to Nurse Sue, mostly about Anna; Mutter and Simon both came and listened. Slept at 7 p.m.; woke at 1 a.m. though, with pain in chest and back and was given something which put me back to sleep.'

24

Wednesday, 11 July 1973

'Woke early. Was got up and out of bed after breakfast and allowed to see Anna. She had sent the blue flowers from Caroline to my ward the previous afternoon! The Registrar and the surgeon who'd taken my skin – both passed by – seemed stunned to see me there – Registrar says: "I told you it would take two or three days – you've gone one better than anyone else!" The surgeon warns that too much movement doesn't help even healing. Anna relatively quiet, dozes mostly, so I go and see children in morning.'

Where they have applied my skin on Anna's legs her limbs seem so thin, like sticks.

25

Thursday, 12 July 1973

'I took Gabriel in to see Anna at 2.15 and only for a very brief moment. Anna pretty quiet after rebandaging and asking us to leave telephone number. Her chin had been covered with a sheet, her chest and legs also – nevertheless the scab wounds on her face worry Gabriel. He shies back and I try to explain where it is getting better already.

'Then we go for a walk on the grass and talk about it.'

26

Friday, 13 July 1973

'9.45 in the evening Gabriel goes to bed. For several moments I wondered how I could possibly read Alice to him, I was so filled with the image of Anna: so terribly thin – "getting thinner before your eyes" as the Registrar put it this evening in pointing out the importance of solids. Her legs – like spindles, and held by actual metal spindles; the gauze hanging on them, draped over them, as though drying in the midday sun ... This is what greeted me this morning when I arrived – at first not able to see her because of the dressings being changed. Very quiet, staring, angry no doubt at the pain. My father had come down from London.

'At first he spoke to her very movingly.

'"I never trusted you," said Anna.

'"You should have," replied my father. "Everyone who knows me trusts me." But then began to talk of how nice it would be to see her again at the country house and in Italy. I was crying, it seemed so much like a last parting; and after he had gone Anna told me she was sorry he had come.

'"Why?"

'"Because he sounded so hopeless."

'Talked a little afterwards with my father. Anna got very fearful meanwhile. Had been asking nurse repeatedly for me. Did not want me to go at lunch, so I stayed all day till 7.45, by which time she was quite sleepy and ready for me to go. Double drip up. The Registrar calls in at 6.15, amused by the way Anna makes him promise to give anaesthetic when changing dressings, but does not look too pleased with legs. "Still a lot of dead skin to come off," he says. "It's going to take a long time." Mutter leaves about 5 p.m.

'As for myself, still in great pain when I walk – and bandages beginning to pong like something tropical! Yesterday even worse...'

27

The pain in my thighs goes on, I have difficulty in sleeping, and it saps the very strength, both moral and physical, I need for Anna. I am reaching the edge.

28

Sunday, 15 July 1973

'Woke latish – telephone call from ward sister saying that Anna is asking for me – but excruciating pain in getting up, so I only got there at ten. They had changed her dressings and she seemed quite peaceful by then – temperature normal, a little more white skin exposed under the lips, but a nasty new gash over left eye as though knocked with something. Managed to give her a lot of milk, soup, and the peaches. In the afternoon the male nurse came to do her observations. I asked how he had come into nursing. Said he had been in merchant navy, then fallen ill, tried this and liked it – too long a chore to do the whole medical training involved in becoming a doctor.

'Anna seemed to be dozing while he spoke and cleaned her mouth (she didn't want him to do dressings and there was some misunderstanding). But later, after tea, she asked for the "seaman" – said she would only eat supper if he did too! I wanted to cry I felt so moved.'

Monday, 16 July 1973

'Woke early, heard Thomas crying, and as Gloria had been awake coughing for much of the night I thought I would try to help by being first up – however painful. Put Thomas on potty. He ran downstairs then in his pyjama top and asked Mrs Trent lots of questions, beginning "What's this for?" – all of which she answers so genuinely and straightforwardly. Gabriel asleep meanwhile.

'Breakfasted but could not manage bike, so had to wait till 9 a.m. and the children in fit condition to come – i.e. wearing shoes.

'When eventually I got there I felt pale and exhausted. Anna seemed dozy, but pleased at least to see me. Nothing more exchanged till Laurie Herbert arrived at almost 12.15. Nurse said she'd give Anna her soup – though Anna insisting that the nurse should first have her own lunch!

'Talked about whole story to Laurie – a salutary telling, for he seemed to listen intently and pick up many associations – the very Christian symbolism – the continual attempt to squeeze through narrow windows, etc., the search for light, for rebirth. Says Anna needs to know of her own courage – be helped to emerge from all this positively.

'Then I took him into Anna's room, but Anna asleep. I think he was very cut. "Worse than one could possibly imagine," he murmured. He left to eat with Gloria and children, while I stayed with Anna. Towards 3 p.m. she seemed to wake a little more, becoming quite bright – and then Gunhilda came in. That really seemed to make the light shine – Gunhilda told story of *Zaun-köpfchen*, and sang a song. Wondering how to feed up Anna a little more.

'Then Anna surprised me – and Gunhilda – by asking about the Community. Gunhilda tells how Laing and Landis want changes, that it should be more open, generous to outsiders! Offer tea, for instance. Bit late in the day!

'"I'm sorry I smashed the Community," says Anna – "No, you did the right thing," replies Gunhilda. "You shook it up at a time when it most needed it."

'But at what cost!

'Nurse gives Anna a beaker of milk, but suddenly will not drink unless *I* have some too! Says she is having it all "easy and comfortable" in her bed while David suffers! Male nurse, about to go, offers to get sauerkraut and wurst. "We think the world of you," he says to Anna, giving her lager and lime she'd just asked for. "Now, no singing mind!"

'Sit on. Laurie comes and I go out – Anna seems anxious that *I* get a rest, not exhausted by her when I say I am afraid too many visitors would tire her.

'Laurie has brought beautiful flowers – so I send him in with them to give to Anna personally. Apparently she asks him to take good care of me!

'Go to local pub. Talk of other things as well – Laing, effect on children, faith . . .

'Return at about 8. Getting dark and Anna quiet. Her teeth white, but when her eyelids close it is only black you see from the left. How can this frail body survive, I wonder – and yet somehow it *will*! Leave, tired, at 10 p.m.

'Remembering yesterday – Laurie's mention of resurrection and the vivid picture I have in my mind of Anna's legs up: crucifixion. Also on responsibility: that the whole problem had been one of responsibility – and yet one cannot act God, cannot take responsibility for *everything*.

'Felt a bit better – told at 9.15 that Anna would be having anaesthetic and new dressings at 11, and meanwhile having linen changed and face done till 10.15. Anna quiet but apparently happy that I was there. Asked if children were dead. I showed her Gabriel's letter. Eyes move slower than usual – but still so powerful!

'Collected by Gloria and children at 11 a.m. and played with them till lunch – both so contented really.

'After lunch, while children "rested", wrote to Landis – probably unfairly, but venting my spleen at Community and helpers and their artificiality – how they used Anna as convenient martyr symbol from the beginning! Poor Landis!

'At hospital shocked to see nose-tube for feeding Anna – so sickened when nurse began to suck out through it that I had to leave. Sister explained necessity – Anna not taking sufficient solids. Then sat with Anna till 6.45. Much of the time apparently asleep (as when physiotherapist came), but actually taking much in. Spoke of Roy, and Roy's child. Calls him "David Roy". "By artificial insemination." When picked up by boys at the fair? Yes. Took 2½ beakers of milk, but major fiasco over orange (my fault for not thinking) and nurse had to use aspirator – most uncomfortable – Anna furious with her, saying only "her" David to come near!

'*Walked* home (without crutches!) and went, after saying goodnight to Gabriel, to the central library.

'Saw Anna, but she seemed fearful – talked of poisoning, and people taking me "upstairs" – left 10.30. Went to bed.'

Wednesday, 18 July 1973

'Woke about 3.30 a.m. and could not sleep for an hour. When I did I started a series of dreams about Anna – about her committing suicide, and appearing in a resurrection scene hours after her death.

'There was one terrible sequence – like a film and in colour – in which I found myself among American troops advancing through a town or village somewhere (it started by seeing a picture of the vehicles and making a film of them – Hondas and limousines just painted another colour). Then the hair-raising ride; and as we drove, troops throwing bombs in doorways –

would make puff of smoke, then mothers would come out pulling babies behind them from the débris – mothers naked, flesh pink, and on their backs and backsides a sort of grey-blue fungus burning their skin – some of the babies already deformed by it – fingers and limbs. How first Anna tried her suicide I cannot now remember – only that as she thought a second time about it and started back across the street, she was immediately run down by a double-decker bus. Report to the police station at the top of a department store; the distress I remember clearly, and talking to a multi-denominational clergyman called then to "assist" – at first I shooed him away, but then called him back, told him I was seeking a different religion from the Anglican, one of the Spirit of God. Then a sort of funeral meeting of relations (all dressed in black) – mostly my family, against my will, insisting it was "necessary" that we all be together and it be done right; (I remember sobbing between my mother's legs) and then Anna appears, on chair, with a bandage on her forehead – talking – and I am so credulous and wanting it to be true that I get up to check verity of her death (certificate etc.) – but people around me make motions and signs signifying that Anna has come to visit only from her other world, and I should accept even this as a mercy.'

'Woke finally later than usual, breakfasted and was taken to hospital by Gloria and Thomas – children seemingly very contented. Mrs Trent departing for a few days, Gabriel making a Fischer-set aeroplane and Thomas trying his hand.

'Anna had just been changed when I got there. After while I noticed that the drips had finished. I told the male nurse and he turned them off. For an hour the drip was left motionless – and then wouldn't start! The other Senior Registrar called in. Looked for another vein, but none immediately available. It was decided to give all fluids via nose-pipe. Then nurse asked him to speak to me – went up to the sitting-room. Sat down. Said sister had told him I wanted a word with him.

'Had a long talk. Told him I knew it was serious and wanted to be kept objectively abreast of things in principle, but in fact got very upset if told that Anna was going to die. Wanted actually only to hear good news. So he explained problems – sudden burning up of muscle, etc., and danger of secondary pack-up of organs, such as digestion. Meanwhile large areas of burned skin uncovered, and even on legs no more skin-laying possible as areas still too messy to take it. Slower than expected – and so little time to play with as body wastes away. Once the body is sealed one can begin to equalize the race between intake and out. "Chances of survival, I would think, are unlikely," he says. "But she has defied the law of averages in coming this far – perhaps she might make it." Would be hospitalized there at least 3–6 months before move to London possible. Rehabilitation – possible amputation of fingers necessary, so badly burned. If she could manage next week, though, she would be over the hump.

'Saw Anna – meanwhile one drip started at least. Told her it is vital to digest what's given, so must relax, etc. Went to lunch – children raced across Common to greet me.

'Rode back to ward on bike. Both drips working now, but Anna in great discomfort with tube – says wants it out – will take drip-feed but not this – and when I try to explain reason so vital, says, "Oh you always want to be right" – just as my father used to when I was a child. Eventually she told me to go away – so I did till after four. Had my own packing bandages removed. When I went back Anna was looking very pale and trembling – comforted to see me I think. Said she didn't want to be a call-girl.

'Little chance of that now!

'Didn't want me to go home for supper and put children to bed. "They can manage all right there for one night, stay with me . . ." So I did – and half an hour later Anna quite happily let me go.

'Returned at 9 p.m. – uncomfortable, mucus in throat, etc. – aspirated – quite horrid to look at. Remains uncomfortable all time I'm there – almost unable to talk – seems to trust night staff though, and asked me to go and be with children at 11 p.m. My own legs still stiff and enervated, tender, where bandages removed. Hope all will be OK. Nurse said I'd never lose traces all my life – quite a shock in itself, though she tried to cover up a little. "I mean you'll always know, though others probably won't be able to see . . ."

'Dream about buying house from family, moving away and converting it – investigated by government/council agent.

'Alarming symbolism! Particularly as my feelings beginning to go beyond simple "save Anna" stage . . .'

29

Thursday, 19 July 1973

'Went in on bike to Anna. Told she was about to have anaesthetic – seemed very parched in throat and still very difficult to talk. A lot of black stuff still in her mouth. The Registrar came round with another consultant (a man of shortish build with bushy beard and rather suffering, intelligent face) who came right up to the head of the bed and asked if she were cold at all. Eventually Anna threw me out for not being able to understand her mumblings.

'Went home for lunch at 12.30 – the anaesthetic delayed owing to non-appearance of anaesthetist, and her hands about to be done. Was told I would be phoned in the afternoon about what would happen – had lunch with children and played with them a bit – talked to Gloria about length of stay, etc.; hospital phoned after 3 p.m. to say no anaesthetic to be given. Arrived to find Anna rather pale and uncomfortable – nurses cleaning her mouth – gave her some water and slowly cleared the mouth and throat till she could speak.

'Sister spoke to me – said yes, was really a case of nursing now. Then male nurse left and the female nurse found it more difficult to clear Anna's throat. Eventually, though, she seemed to go into a fitful sleep (with her left hand, plastic-bagged, shaking like a leaf beside her head). She awoke seemingly much refreshed. Did not want me to go home, so had my supper there – but she didn't like my talking to the nurse and told me off in no uncertain manner! Undoubtedly it is her wit and tenacity have brought her through.

'Alarmed to read in textbook that burns of more than a certain

181

percentage have no chance of survival – and surgeons not recommended to prolong life at start of hospital treatment.

'Will she live? Can she live? Still so impossible to tell – statistically impossible: yet so far she survives.

'Eventually got angry with me again for talking to nurse (seemed to distrust her) and told me not to come for a day.

'Yet we are all dying – and time is an illusion.'

'"*Du kannst nach Hause gehen – die Früchte deiner Arbeit ausüben* [you can go home now – reap the rewards of your work]."

'Dream: chasing someone with the police and Peter – at top of a sort of Empire State Building, of steps; coming down get frightened, have to go backwards – something to do with death.'

The passage in the book, *Burns and their Treatment* by Muir and Barclay, reads:

HOPELESS CASES

The facilities available for the treatment of burns shock make it possible for almost all patients, no matter how severe their injuries are, to survive through the shock period. In the present state of our knowledge, however, patients with burns above a critical size invariably succumb after having lived in great pain and misery for a few days or weeks.

The relationship between increasing age and the decreasing size of burn which will be fatal has already been discussed in Chapter 1, and a simplified form of 'probability chart' is reproduced in Fig. 20.

The surgeon will sometimes be faced with the situation where the age of the patient and the size of his burn put him in the category where recovery is unknown. The question must then be asked whether it is not more humane to give only symptomatic treatment and to make the patient as comfortable as possible, while awaiting the inevitable end, than to persevere with resuscitation regardless of the outcome. We believe that this is a proper question for the surgeon to ask himself and that when the indications are clear it is his duty to withhold active resuscitation, but to give as much symptomatic relief as possible.

According to the Muir Barclay chart in their book, Anna might have a good chance of recovery if her burns do not exceed

37% of her total body. Between 37% and 50% she would have a 'small chance of recovery'. Above 50% she is doomed to die.

Anna's burns exceed 75%.

30

Friday, 20 July 1973

'Soaked off gauze in bath – slow, but not as painful as I supposed, since it was I who was inflicting the pain. Arrived at 11 a.m. – Anna still very weak, only able to say a few words – very pale – respirations high. Went to sleep and I left at 12.30. The Registrar says no change really. Not keeping down stomach foods, though. Returned after lunch to be told that she would be given an anaesthetic at three. Seemed still very uncomfortable, face going purple-blue; having blood now by drip. Nurse aspirates all food – but Anna coughs and one wonders how she can be given anaesthetic in this condition. After reading the surgical book on burns yesterday I feel horrified, as never before, by the sheer extent and damage. Will she ever walk again? Ever make love? Amputation of fingers? Oh, it is horrible. Feel I cannot cope any longer with my own thoughts. Go home at 3 p.m. when nurses arrive and spend an hour ruminating in my room. At 4 p.m. Dan and Patty arrive – start talking – then Laurie – have tea with children. Discussion starts – vent all my resentment and feelings of blame. Cover whole spectrum of schizophrenia, etc. Patty suggests taking over for a little while while I go away. Might well be answer.

'They leave at 8 p.m., and Laurie and I are alone for supper once Gabriel settles. We talk about writing poetry, and Anna; the need to have fun – not to apportion blame, but to find one's smaller place in the universe – not take upon oneself God's role, which is what I was doing really – so exhausted by everything.'

31

Saturday, 21 July 1973

'Went in morning: Anna still very weak and finding it almost impossible to talk. But still cheerful – smile for Mrs Fröhlich, the cleaner – mentioned baby – whose, I wondered. Then I said I wanted to go away for a day or two to regain a little strength for the coming months. Anna seemed not keen. Nor was the nursing staff after lunch when I told them of my plan. When I said Patty would be coming to sit in for me, Anna suddenly said, relatively clearly: "Tell Patty I'm not going back there." When I asked whether "there" meant "madness" she seemed to nod; yet when I asked if it was a physical, geographical place she also nodded. Said it several times.

'"Was it too awful?" I asked; and her whole face said yes. On the other hand she seemed definitely to want Patty to come – or showed pleasure at the thought.

'Then in the afternoon Landis rang and said he would come instead. He arrived at 7.45 and I went home and wrote newspaper piece. Anna very weak, though showing good response to Roy.

'He came over then at 11 p.m. and we talked until 4 a.m. – of guilt, of helpers, of irresponsibility, alternatives, other cases ... Felt clearly my own uptightness and distrust of others – not good.'

32

Sunday, 22 July 1973

'Went to the hospital to collect Roy at 8 a.m. – discussed nose-tube; took him to the station. At hospital Anna not very different from yesterday; frightened-looking, as Roy had noticed – so I just talked to her of the children. The nurse cleaned her mouth, but she could not manage to speak. Eyes still perfect deep brown, clear – only tears at corner – almost stronger than the day before. They changed bed and dressings at eleven, so I went home early and finished article and instructions to editor. After lunch went back to Anna. Male nurse had brought in cassette tape-recorder and Anna seemed quite pleased and grateful. Apparently he had asked her favourite music and recorded it at home. Still breathing very very fast as though either afraid or short-winded ... but after the nurse had again cleaned her mouth and I had given her some orange she began to speak quite loudly. Very difficult to make out words ... Something like: "I have always loved you" – I asked if that was what she meant and she nodded – confirmed a little later when I asked if she really did. "But love isn't always enough in this world," was all I could say; yet that within love I had never loved anyone as I had her. "Poor David," she also seemed to be trying to say. She swung her right leg a great deal, suspended from the overhead frame, and stared intently at the pictures of the children I had stuck there – as though drawing a great deal of succour from them. Then she began talking of "baby" – I said did she mean the one she thought she was carrying? She nodded. But that's you, the baby, I pointed out gently. She looked puzzled and shook her head a little – interrupted by news that Gunhilda had come.

'I went into town for the evening. The cinemas were booked out, so I wandered a little in the streets of the old quarter; then drove into the country, without stopping, without knowing where I was going. It was dusk when I reached the great, ruined abbey.'

33

Monday, 23 July 1973

Woke finally before 8 a.m. after uncomfortable night in the van – cold and continually slipping off mattress.

Picked way over and beneath the ruined abbey then, thinking of its size, its self-sufficiency: an example of a real community, devoted to spiritual and religious aims and not relying – as so many others – on generosity of others. Related to Laurie's book and its anti-money theme very extraordinarily. Thought how temporal greed (under Henry VIII) had crushed it: and that one must come to see 'money' as a sort of interval in man's history.

Drove back mid-morning.

'At hospital (11.30 a.m.) Anna "out" and oxygen cylinders by the bed. Nurse says that she had had anaesthetic and that the dressings on her legs had been changed, and more of my skin put on. Suggested I come after lunch. At home there was a note from Gunhilda saying had returned to London as no Bed and Breakfast available. Gave Gabriel and Thomas their presents from my trip – Thomas almost asleep on Gloria's lap, Gabriel playing with neighbour's boy.

'Worked on layout for newspaper page. After lunch rewrote a little, posted to typist. Rang paper, then cycled to hospital. There Anna very much awake: breathing strongly but very fast – mouth extraordinarily clean and fresh. Seemed to recognize me, though eyes having difficulty in staying down – often sliding upwards. Tried to tell me something, her whole head shaking: looked intently at pictures of children, and particularly Gabriel's letters to her – which I read aloud, telling her not to worry about the children, that they were well and very close by – playing out on the common, both in new shoes, and Thomas stomping in puddles in his boots. Had to read the letter again and again – seemed as though Anna was trying to say the children's names and: "Read . . . letter."

'Gave her water. But male nurse says only sips advisable as she has difficulty with mucus etc., in throat. Calmed her a little, shaded her eyes and tried to encourage her to sleep, saying there would be time to talk, but now she must keep all her strength . . .

'The flowers, bought only on Saturday evening, had already begun to wilt – all of them I noticed suddenly – as though someone had sprayed them with something. I could not but be aware of an omen, with Anna so very weak. Anaesthetic apparently not given owing to her condition, only form of ether and then relaxing injection lasting an hour. Sister says her condition "worst so far". Keeps saying that. Says I should stay in the ward if I wish, the waiting-room couch will be made up. Agreed to see how things go.

186

'At one point I had felt an urge to go into town to see the film I'd missed previous night, but (7.30 p.m.) Anna still waking from snatches of snoring-like sleep every few minutes. Seems to have pain or something under left shoulder, tipping hand towards me. Eyes sliding more and more upwards – gradually impossible to bring them down. Sitting there without a book suddenly I became aware of what I was really missing . . .

'Read Book of Job, first chapter, as Anna seemed to say yes when I asked her – Roy had recommended it when I deposited him at the station, reminded of Job's temptations and his implacable faith: and the more and more painful the trial Satan imposes.

'About 9 p.m. I asked sister to call the vicar. He came immediately, and we said prayers. Tried to get Anna to open her eyes and look at me when I told her the intention. Then Simon asked: "Would you like me to pray?" She seemed briefly to nod her head in acknowledgment or to say yes. We knelt.

'Afterwards Simon stayed for over an hour while we talked of God, of the need not to usurp His place. Also of the abbey, of money, of the need for the Church to become more political. Anna began to stir her head agitatedly (not at what we were saying, though, I think), and when I caressed her hair with my fingers she seemed – as she had done in the evening – to push her head upwards, against the palm of my hand . . .

'Simon left about 11 p.m. I talked to the staff nurse about acupuncture – I can't remember how it came up. She had just aspirated 30mls from the stomach tube and put in a small feed, had left me reading, and then there we were standing on each side of the bed . . . We talked about the spirit as an element of healing. I was almost angry, didn't want to argue over Anna's sick body. Then I asked about whether I should go home or not – and we stood away from the bed. She said it was up to me, and I asked what was likely to happen in the next few days.

'"She will probably just . . .", and she motioned with her hand, signifying sinking.

'I asked what that meant: wouldn't something fail? She shook her head. "Not necessarily." She seemed to want to explain as best she could, but to be unable, or wary in choosing words lest she upset me. I urged her to be honest – asked how long Anna could continue in present condition. Nurse shook her head – "She could last till morning" – then stopped herself as though she had put it too bluntly. "No, no," I urged her again. "I want you to tell me the truth."

'We discussed whether it was better for me to go home or to stay in the ward waiting-room. On balance, she thought the waiting-room. She went to get pillows, but blanket and pillow already there. She said she would call me if Anna's condition changed at all.

'It was about midnight now. I wondered momentarily if – as at the farm – I would be guilty of deserting Anna if I went to sleep; but it seemed too important for me to get some sleep if I was to cope with whatever might happen later.

'Got onto my knees and began to pray – as once when a child. Only the prayer was difficult.

'"Oh God . . . Oh God . . . I don't know what to ask of you . . . I don't know what is best for Anna . . . But I beg you to give me courage to cope with what you decide, whether it be Anna's death or her rebirth in recovery.

'"And forgive, dear God, my awful failings – my weakness, my superficiality – all those failings where in contrast Anna possesses such strength . . . Amen."

'I lay down, but could not sleep for a long while. At one point the settee began to tremble, and I wondered whether that were not a transference, but no one came. Eventually I slipped away into sleep.

'When I awoke it was dark: and above me, as I was turning, was a dark figure. I was frightened and shrank back.

'It was the little night sister.

'She apologized, and then said: "I'm afraid I've got some bad news. Your wife passed away a few minutes ago."

'I held her hand as she stood there, buried my head against her. Then she sat down, insisting I wait until the doctor came before going in. She explained that it had happened "quite, quite peacefully". The nurse, who had stayed with her, had left to replace the saline bottle, and when she came back Anna seemed to have gone.

'It seemed impossible to digest – mind-leaping, incredulous, because unimaginable. We talked; then I asked if the vicar could be called.

'It was 2 a.m., and 2.30 by the time Simon was there. I told him what had happened. Later the doctor called. Presumably death was confirmed, but sister wanted to "tidy" Anna up – taking out pins, according to nurse.

'Finally sister returned and led me in. Anna was covered completely by a white sheet – her legs now at rest. The little sister ("You can come now, deary," she had said colloquially at the end of the ward) pulled back the top end of the sheet.

'The sight caused me to start. The face was white where the good skin showed – a deathly white like alabaster, with the mouth very slightly open and the eyelids not completely closed. I kissed her forehead, Simon went the other side – and we prayed, kneeling.

'"Oh Lord, look down upon this Thy servant Anna ..."

'We prayed for strength for me and the children too: and then also I said a prayer.

'"Oh dear, dear God ... thank you for giving Anna the courage, the chance to live for these past five weeks. Thank you for permitting her a chance to show her true spirit of goodness, of concern for others, her generosity and thought. I beg that you will give me the courage to act according to that example, never to forget her goodness and love ... Amen.'

'I kissed her twice on the forehead – felt the coldness of the skin. Under the sheet the shoulders were going alabaster white too.

'I picked up the prayer book Simon had lent me; I left the Bible beside Anna. I gathered my jacket off the chair, looked round once again – and left. Simon then brought me home. I embraced him – as I had the night nurse who had been so good.

'"Come and see us again," she had said. "Not that you will want to." And I kissed her cheek, held her shoulders, thanked her for what she had done, for her goodness towards Anna.

'The smell I can still remember – like a sweet brine.'

Anna is dead. Her trial is over.

More about Penguins
and Pelicans